NIXON'S HOROSCOPE

by
Lynne Palmer

TABLE OF CONTENTS

Nixon's Horoscope

ISBN-13:
978-1500967024

ISBN-10:
1500967025

Published by:

Lynne Palmer
Toll Free: 1-800-615-3352
Web Site: www.lynnepalmer.com
Email: lynnepalmer@lynnepalmer.com

Printed and bound in the United States of America

WORKS BY LYNNE PALMER

BOOKS

ABC Chart Erection
ABC Major Progressions
ABC Chart Reading
Pluto Daily Ephemeris (1900-2000)
Horoscope of Billy Rose

RECORD ALBUM

Cast And Read Your Horoscope

ACKNOWLEDGEMENTS

Grateful acknowledgement is made to the following people who assisted with the typing: Maria Sample, Darlene Larson and Kathy Goody; and a special thanks to my dear friend and an excellent astrologer Amanda Rosenberg, who, not only did most of the typing in it's early stage, but whose invaluable assistance I greatly appreciated for helping me at every needed moment.

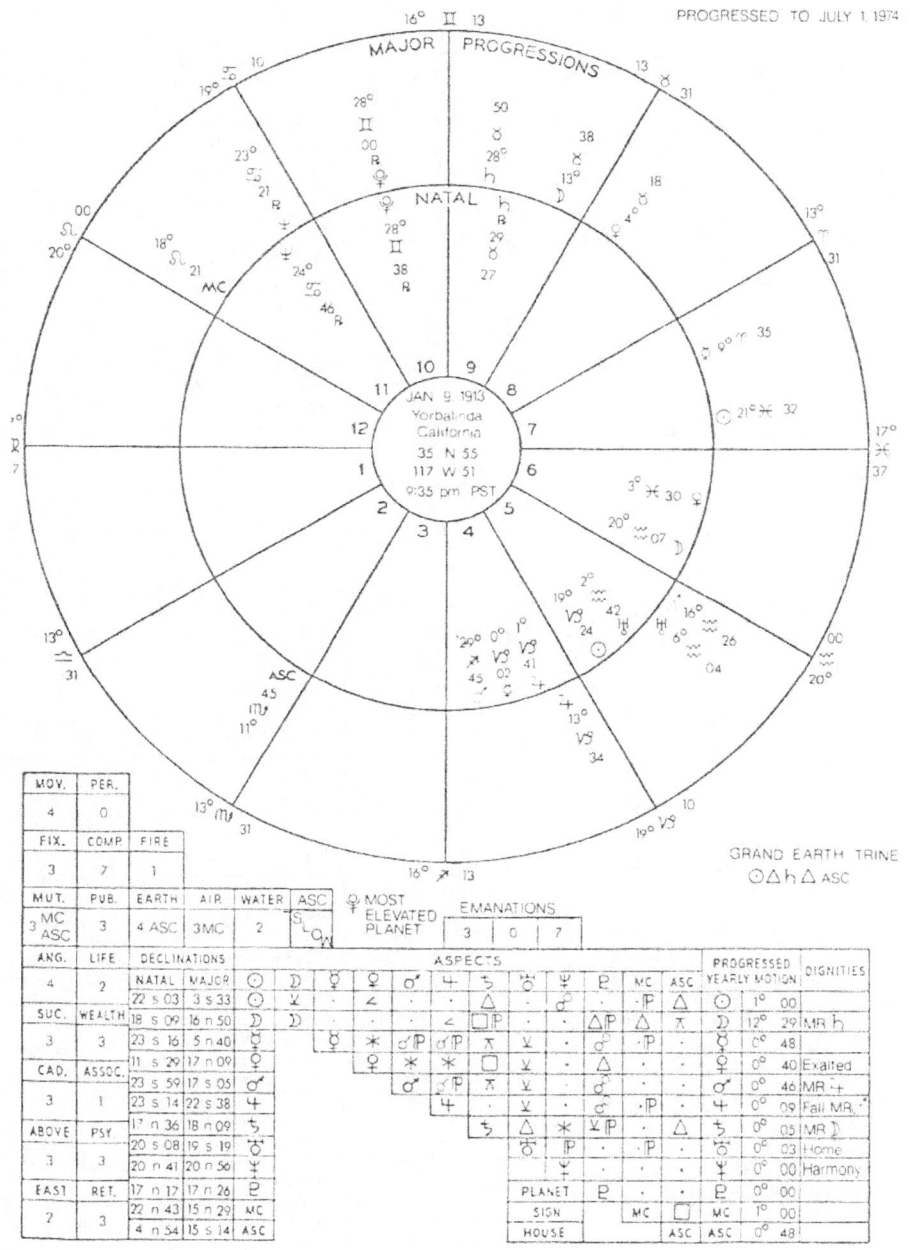

MAJOR PROGRESSIONS

NATAL

JAN 9 1913
Yorbalinda
California
35 N 55
117 W 51
9:35 pm PST

GRAND EARTH TRINE
☉△ ♄ △ ASC

MOV.	PER.																					
4	0																					

FIX.	COMP	FIRE
3	7	1

MUT.	PUB.	EARTH	AIR	WATER	ASC
3 MC ASC	3	4 ASC	3 MC	2	

♀ MOST ELEVATED PLANET

EMANATIONS		
3	0	7

ANG.	LIFE	DECLINATIONS							ASPECTS								PROGRESSED YEARLY MOTION		DIGNITIES
4	2	NATAL	MAJOR	☉	☽	☿	♀	♂	♃	♄	♅	♆	♇	MC	ASC		☉	1° 00	
		22 s 03	3 s 33	☉	⚹		∠		.	.	.	.	P	△			☽	12° 29	MR ♄
SUC.	WEALTH	18 s 09	16 n 50	☽	☽	.	.	.	∠	□ P		△ P	△	⊼			☿	0° 48	
3	3	23 s 16	5 n 40	☿	☿	⚹	♂ P	♂ P	⊼	☿	.	♂	. P	.		♀	0° 40	Exalted
CAD.	ASSOC.	11 s 29	17 n 09	♀		⚹	⚹	□	☿	.	△	.	.			♂	0° 46	MR ♃
3	1	23 s 59	17 s 05	♂		♂	⚹ P	⊼	☿	.	♂	. P	.			♃	0° 09	Fall MR
ABOVE	PSY.	23 s 14	22 s 38	♃			♃			☿	.	♂	. P			♄	0° 05	MR ☽
3	3	17 n 36	18 n 09	♄				♄	△	⚹	☿ P	.	△			♅	0° 03	Home
EAST	RET.	20 s 08	19 s 19	♅					♅	P	.	.	. P			♆	0° 00	Harmony
2	3	20 n 41	20 n 56	♆						♆	.	.	.					
		17 n 17	17 n 26	♇							PLANET	♇	.		P	♇	0° 00	
		22 n 43	15 n 29	MC							SIGN		MC	□	MC	1° 00	
		4 n 54	15 s 14	ASC							HOUSE			ASC	ASC	0° 48	

iv

MAJOR PROGRESSED ASPECTS

Starts July 20, 1974	☉r $\overline{\pi}$ᵖ MСp	Peak – July 21, 1975
Starts Apr. 26, 1975	☉p ⚷△ Ψp	Peak – Apr. 22, 1976
Starts Oct. 1, 1976	☉p ⚷△ Ψr	Peak – Oct. 1, 1977
Started Apr. 17, 1941	☉r ℙᴺ ♃p	Peak – never
Starts Sept. 21, 1976	☿r $\overline{\pi}$ ♄p	Peak – years
Started Nov. 17, 1971	♀p ℙ△ ♀p	Peak – Oct. 29, 1974
Started June, 1972	♀p ℙ□ ♄r	Peak – Apr. 15, 1975
In orb for years	♀p ℙ□ ♄p.	Peak – Feb. 17, 1977
Starts Oct. 14, 1975	♀p □ᵛ ♅p	Peak – June, 1977
Started July 7, 1973	♂p ∠ℙ ♃r	Peak – Oct. 22, 1974
Starts Sept. 22, 1974	♂p $\overline{\pi}$ᴺ Asc r	Peak – Jan. 8, 1976
Started Apr. 17, 1973	♂r $\overline{\pi}$ ♄p	Peak – June 17, 1985
Starts Oct. 22, 1975	♂p ℙᴺ Asc p	Peak – years
Starts Oct. 9, 1975	♃p ⚹ᴺ Asc p	Peak – Apr. 17, 1977
Started Apr. 17, 1966	♃p ⚻ᴺ ♄ p	Peak – May 17, 1978
Always has been in orb	♄r ℙᵛ ♀ p	never peaks
Started Apr. 17, 1920	♄r ⚻ᵛ ♀ p	(App. Sep. in for yrs)
Starts Oct. 29, 1974	♀p ⚻ᴺ Asc p	Peak – Jan. 31, 1976
Starts Aug. 21, 1975	♀r ⚻ᴺ Asc p	Peak – Nov. 23, 1976

MC into 12th house – Feb. 26, 1976

Asc into 3rd house – Sept. 28, 1976

MAJOR PROGRESSED MOON ASPECTS

Started July, 1974	$☽_p \overset{N}{\mathbb{P}} ♆_r$	Peak – Oct. 24, 1974
Started May, 1974	$☽_p \overset{N}{\mathbb{P}} ♆_p$	Peak – Nov. 15, 1974
Starts Oct. 28, 1974	$☽_p \overset{\triangle}{\square} MC_p$	Peak – Nov. 28, 1974
Starts Nov. 17, 1974	$☽_p \overset{⊻}{\triangle} ☉_r$	Peak – Dec. 17, 1974
Starts Aug., 1974	$☽_p \overset{⊻}{\mathbb{P}} ☉_r$	Peak – Feb. 20, 1975
Starts Feb. 8, 1975	$☽_p \overset{⊻}{⚹} ☉_p$	Peak – Mar. 8, 1975
Starts Mar. 9, 1975	$☽_p \overset{N}{⚹} ♆_p$	Peak – Apr. 9, 1975
Starts Oct., 1974	$☽_p \overset{\angle}{\mathbb{P}} ♃_p$	Peak – Apr. 13, 1975
Starts Oct., 1974	$☽_p \overset{\triangle}{\mathbb{P}} MC_r$	Peak – Apr. 24, 1975
Starts Apr. 20, 1975	$☽_p \overset{N}{⚹} ♆_r$	Peak – May 20, 1975
Starts May 4, 1975	$☽_p \overset{N}{\angle} ☿_p$	Peak – June 4, 1975
Starts Dec., 1974	$☽_p \overset{\angle}{\mathbb{P}} ♃_r$	Peak – June 10, 1975
Starts Dec., 1974	$☽_p \overset{N}{\mathbb{P}} ☿_r$	Peak – June 15, 1975
Starts July 6, 1975	$☽_p \overset{\square p}{☌} ♄_r$	Peak – Aug. 6, 1975
Starts July 21, 1975	$☽_p \overset{\triangle p}{⊻} ♇_p$	Peak – Aug. 21, 1975
Starts Feb., 1975	$☽_p \overset{N}{\mathbb{P}} ♂_r$	Peak – Aug. 24, 1975
Starts Aug. 8, 1975	$☽_p \overset{\triangle p}{⊻} ♇_r$	Peak – Sept. 8, 1975
Starts Aug. 16, 1975	$☽_p \overset{\square p}{☌} ♄_p$	Peak – Sept. 16, 1975
Starts Sept. 10, 1975	$☽_p \overset{N}{⚻} ♂_r$	Peak – Oct. 10, 1975
	$☽_p$ into ♊	– Oct. 17, 1975
Starts Sept. 17, 1975	$☽_p \overset{N}{⚻} ☿_r$	Peak – Oct. 17, 1975

Starts Nov. 3, 1975	☽ₚ ⚻ ♃ᵣ	Peak – Dec. 3, 1975
Starts Dec. 1, 1975	☽ₚ △(N) ♅⚥ᵣ	Peak – Jan. 1, 1976
Starts Dec. 23, 1975	☽ₚ □(N) ♀ᵣ	Peak – Jan. 23, 1976
Starts Jan. 18, 1976	☽ₚ ☌(v) ☉ᵣ	Peak – Feb. 18, 1976
Starts Feb. 18, 1976	☽ₚ ⅄(N) ♀ₚ	Peak – Mar. 18, 1976
Starts Mar. 8, 1976	☽ₚ △(N) ♅⚥ₚ	Peak – Apr. 8, 1976
Started Apr. 11, 1975	☽ᵣ ☍(△) MCₚ	Peak – Apr. 11, 1976
Starts May 7, 1976	☽ₚ ∠(N) ♆ₚ	Peak – June 7, 1976
Starts June 18, 1976	☽ₚ ∠(N) ♆ᵣ	Peak – July 18, 1976
Starts July 21, 1976	☽ₚ ✶(N) ☿ₚ	Peak – Aug. 21, 1976
Starts Oct. 1, 1976	☽ₚ ⚻(⫪) Ascₚ	Peak – Nov. 1, 1976
Starts Oct. 10, 1976	☽ₚ ⚻ ♃ₚ	Peak – Nov. 10, 1976
Starts Dec. 15, 1976	☽ₚ ☍(△) MCᵣ	Peak – Jan. 15, 1977
	☽ₚ into 10th house	– Jan. 15, 1977
Started Mar. 11, 1974	☽ᵣ ⇂↾(N) ♀ₚ	Peak – few years
Always has been in orb	☽ᵣ ⇂↾(△ₚ) ♀⯑ₚ	Peak – never

vii

FOREWORD

On page iv there is a copy of Nixon's horoscope. The small center circle in the middle represents the earth. The next circle out is where the planets fall in his natal chart at the exact moment of birth. The last circle out is where the planets are by Major Progression for July 1, 1974.

The twelve segments on the chart represent various departments of life, called *HOUSES* in astrology. Each area rules more than one phase of life. The houses are divided by house cusp dividing lines which appear like twelve spokes of a wheel. On the outer edge of each (the house cusp) is a sign of the zodiac.

The signs of the zodiac are ruled by one, or two, planets. If a house in a chart is empty, it still has a meaning. One takes the sign on the house cusp, the planet, or planets, that rule it; this will give you the meaning of the empty house. The house a planet is actually located in, is more important than the empty area it rules by sign alone.

The ten planets each signify various mannerisms of thinking and acting, which, in turn, attracts events into one's life. It depends upon the aspects made to them, whether one will use the energy harmoniously or inharmoniously.

An aspect is the distance apart between two planets. Some distances are favorable, others, unfavorable; some are fair.

One may attract good chances and fortune under the harmonious aspects; problems, difficulties and trouble under the inharmonious ones; and a "blah" or intensified feeling under some of the neutral (fair) aspects.

NOTE: For the meanings of the houses, planets and aspects (in detail) see Lynne Palmer's ABC Chart Reading book.

* * *

This book is designed for a student who wants to learn more about chart reading. If one wants to learn how to read the progressions, see said chapter. It's also written for a person who desires to skip the technical points, and read about Nixon only.

Part One deals with an analysis of his character (the natal chart)—what he's like. It takes a variety of traits, good and bad, to make a complete individual. This is represented by a variety of aspects in a chart, harmonious and inharmonious; with them, a person acts in a particular manner.

I have written all of the different sides to Nixon's personality. He may appear like a Jekyll and Hyde; also, he may feel that he is! Not all of the traits (planets) will be activated in one day.

Richard Nixon may be kind under one aspect; temperamental under another; yet, sneaky under another one. With different people, he may use various traits. Therefore, there are no contradictions in this book.

Part Two deals with Nixon's present and future aspects—called *Major Progressions*. These are the important events which can be attracted, and never forgotten.

Dates and different types of energies overlap each other. Part of the time, Nixon may use the harmonious aspects and attract favorable events; at other moments, he may use the discordant aspect and have a problem on his hands. It is up to Nixon to channel the energy in the direction he chooses.

There are no contradictions in Part Two. For example, the following: Under a harmonious aspect (Venus progressed Parallel Pluto progressed-natal trine aspect), Nixon may spend the taxpayer's money on luxury gifts for those in foreign nations. He may feel wonderful in so doing, and the results may be in his favor as far as the recipient of the present is concerned.

However, under a discordant aspect (Mars progressed Semi-square Jupiter natal-natal Conjunction and Parallel aspect) this excessive spending will create problems with the public, and Nixon may secretly worry about it. In other words, one side of him is happy that he spent the money, but another side is unhappy. Also, the receiver of the gift is pleased and feels friendly toward Nixon. However, the public is not pleased and feels unfriendly toward him.

* * *

Part Three deals with the monthly Moon aspects. All of every one's life, there are these Moon aspects. They bring minor events, and show a person's emotional reactions to major events and to daily occurrences.

The mood Nixon can be in every month is shown by these aspects. They can tie in with the way he feels and acts under the major events (major progressions). As a rule, six months after a Moon aspect leaves the chart, the event, or aspect, is forgotten.

* * *

I have tried to be objective in this book. In no way, did I write my own personal opinion of Nixon. Everything is based upon his chart, using only astrological meanings of the planets, houses and aspects.

Torrance, California
July 31, 1974   *LYNNE PALMER*

HOW TO READ MAJOR PROGRESSIONS
USING THE FINAL SHEET

EXPLANATION OF THE FINAL SHEET

NOTE: Nixon's Final Sheet is on pages v-vii. The complete explanation of how to mathematically arrive at a Final Sheet, and it's purpose, is explained in detail in Lynne Palmer's *ABC Major Progressions* book. However, on these pages are some brief explanatory notes which are not, in their entirety, in the other book.

The aspects are listed in planetary section. The process of elimination has been used; therefore, an aspect is not repeated from one area to another.

The starting date of the aspect is ALWAYS listed on the left side; the aspect in the middle; the peak date to the right of the aspect.

Each aspect, in a planet's section, is listed according to their peak date order (not the starting date order). The reading is given in peak date order and one only has to glance at the right hand side of the page to see which aspect will be mentioned first.

If you wish to list them in peak date order (and not in a planetary section), you may. My reason for the planetary section, in peak date order (in each section), is given in my *ABC Major Progressions* book.

* * *

In Parts Two and Three, you will notice that the natal aspect which the progressed planet stimulates is mentioned. On the Final Sheet, pages iv-vi, you will see that the natal aspect is written above the progressed aspect. The purpose, for so doing, is explained in the *ABC Major Progressions* book.

* * *

Many planets move so slow, by major progression—the declination (Parallel aspect)—that it can possibly take 200 years for a peak to be reached; therefore, "Never Peaks" written on the Final Sheet implies exactly what it says.

* * *

On the Final Sheet, you will notice the following: app, sep, in for years. This means that the planets are *applying* toward a peak, then *separate*, but remain in the chart for years.

In this case, the planet is increasing (applying) in degrees and minutes to make an aspect; however, it doesn't quite reach a peak because it goes retrograde (decreases in degrees and minutes). As it moves retrograde, the planet stays within a one degree orb of an aspect for years.

In Nixon's horoscope, this occurs with a Mars and ASC aspect by major progression (see page v—the Final Sheet, the Mars sections). It so happens, in his chart, that the one Mars ASC aspect is reinforced with additional energy by another aspect involving Mars and the ASC.

* * *

Nixon's chart has been progressed to July 1, 1974—this date is called the calendar date. On the Final Sheet, pages v-vii, to the left of some aspects are the "in orb" dates. This implies that the planets were in orb of a one degree aspect PRIOR to the calendar date.

By listing in orb to the left, one can tell at a quick glance those aspects which have been in for a while, or before the calendar date of July 1, 1974.

* * *

To save space, the dates the aspects LEAVE Nixon's chart are NOT LISTED on the Final Sheet; however, some are mentioned in Parts One and Two at the beginning of each aspect.

* * *

Many times, the following occurs: If there are mostly harmonious aspects under the major progressions and mostly discordant aspects under the Moon progressions, the individual is likely to not take advantage of the favorable opportunities because his moods and emotions lead him into goofing.

If there are mostly discordant aspects under the major progressions and mostly harmonious aspects under the Moon progressions, the individual is likely to take action and struggle to overcome any discord present. The person's emotional reactions are so pleasant that any negative influence (under the major progressed inharmony) is not even noticed. This type of thinking is apt to lead the person toward success.

* * *

Another reason that the Final Sheet has everything listed on three pages is because it makes it easier to ascertain when a major progressed Moon aspect will tie-up with a major progressed planet to give the timing of when an event can occur.

For instance: The progressed Sun Square natal Mercury. The peak of the aspect is January 1975. In December 1974, the progressed Moon peaks to a

Semi-square to the natal Sun and a Square to the progressed Mercury. (Note: This is all Sun, Mercury energy and does not have to directly hit the Sun progressed or natal Mercury—as in the progressed aspect.)

These progressed Moon aspects both occur ONE MONTH PRIOR to the major progressed Sun Square natal Mercury; therefore, the most likely time for the event to transpire will be in December of 1974, rather than the peak date month of January 1975.

NOTE: The preceding is an example and is not Nixon's chart.

* * *

To avoid repetition when giving the reading it's best to double-up on the peak dates of an aspect; especially with the Major Progressed Moon aspects.

For example: In Nixon's chart the progressed Moon will be Trine the natal Uranus from December 1, 1975 to January 1, 1976. This aspect is repeated from March 8, 1976 to April 8, 1976.

During the preceding time period, Nixon has two other progressed Moon aspects; therefore, by doubling-up on the Moon, Uranus dates and mentioning them together, repetition is avoided. Later, one can return to the other two Moon aspects which are in-between the two Moon, Uranus aspects. By glancing at the dates in Parts Two and Three you will see how this was done.

* * *

For a complete reading of the progressions, take into account the meanings of the planets, aspects (both natal and progressed) and the houses involved.

The houses imply the natal ones which are stimulated (the natal position of the planet), the house where the planet is by major progression and the houses ruled by a planet because of the zodiacal sign on the house cusp (each sign has a planet that rules it).

The planet, aspect and houses are all tied together as I have done in Parts Two and Three with Nixon's chart. For the detailed meanings of the planets, aspects and houses see my book *ABC Chart Reading.*

* * *

The Starting Date of an Aspect is when two planets (including the natal and progressed MC and ASC) are exactly *one degree and zero minutes* apart (regardless of the zodiacal sign they are in). This means that they will start to apply (move) toward one another.

The Peak Date of an Aspect is when two planets (including the natal and progressed MC and ASC) are exactly the *same degree and same minute* (0°00') apart (regardless of the zodiacal sign they are in). This implies that they have reached an impact (peak, a perfect figure, or most power).

The Leaving Date of an Aspect is when two planets (including the natal and progressed MC and ASC) are exactly *one degree and one minute* apart (regardless of the zodiacal sign they are in). This means that they have gone out of orb (moved away from one another).

A Separating Aspect implies that the planets have reached a peak and are decreasing (moving away from each other). They start to separate when they are *the same degree* (0°) and *one minute past* the peak figure of 0°00'.

* * *

Most major events transpire anytime from the starting date to the peak date. Each aspect works differently; each reacts in his own manner.

Usually when an aspect first starts, the individual notices, feels or attracts specific events in relation to the planets, aspects and houses. Many times, these activities will subside (appear to have settled down), only to suddenly be stirred into action one or two months before a peak date, or around the peak date period. However, there are people, who have events occur *all of the time an aspect is in*.

As the energies of the planets build and approach a peak, a stronger force is felt with each passing day until the impact (peak) is reached. Some aspects are more powerful than others; thereby, bringing more activity and attention to them.

Those aspects with the *least power* are: The Inconjunct and Semi-sextile; *fair power*, the Sextile, Semi-square, Sesqui-square; *gradual intensified power*, the Parallel; *real strong power*, the Square and Trine; the *most and strongest power*, the Opposition and Conjunction.

Once a peak has been reached, events can still occur until the aspect has left the chart. Many times, a minor progressed aspect, transit, or another major progressed planet, will temporarily hit them so they are back in action.

* * *

An aspect that has always been in a chart (since the birth of the individual) will not be as noticeable as a new aspect starting. As a rule, one becomes accustomed to the aspect that has always been in; therefore, it isn't generally noticed until the last several years before it peaks (if it reaches a peak). There are exceptions to this which are dependent upon the aspect and how the person has handled it.

* * *

UNDERSTANDING PROGRESSIONS

When giving a reading, the astrologer must always be objective. One should never give a reading expressing one's own opinions on how a person should act. The astrologer can suggest changes which will bring greater harmony into the life, but this should always be *based* upon what is *good for the individual in question* based upon the person's horoscope. The chart will show what is desired.

* * *

Changes can occur in the life when a planet changes signs or houses; also, under a Mercury or Uranus aspect: the latter, mostly when the ASC is involved in the aspect. For instance: one suddenly becomes money orientated. This may be due to a major progressed planet (or the progressed ASC) having entered the 2nd house of money; or, an aspect (by Major Progression) is in with a planet which rules the 2nd house.

* * *

A person's attitude, or thinking, may alter. This may be due to a planet changing signs, or a new aspect has entered the chart. The latter can occur when there is no aspect in the natal chart between two planets.

In a case like this, the person tends to feel as if a foreign substance has entered his body. Many times, one will say, "I have changed. I'm a different person than before."

The new aspect gives the individual new traits to express. As a rule, when it's a discordant aspect, one experiences difficulty with people because of a lack of knowledge in how to handle this new aspect in a constructive manner.

* * *

An aspect gives a person a desire to become involved in a particular activity. A lack of interest in a specific area, may denote the lack of an aspect in this direction.

A good example is of one who's not interested in marriage (because there's no aspect, by major progression, to the 7th house). Suddenly, the person becomes interested in being a legal mate to another (this feeling may be in regardless of whether the individual has someone in mind or not). The reason the party now wants to marry is because there is an aspect by major progression to the 7th house of marriage. Whether the person actually takes the trip to the altar will be dependent upon the conditioning of the individual, the environment within which he moves, and the ability to attract a partner.

* * *

If an individual doesn't have many aspects in his chart during a specific time period, he may not be as active as he has been when he was loaded with aspects. Also, he may feel tired, energyless, bored, and not have much initiative. It's possible that the person has overworked in previous years and now needs a rest.

Major progressed Sun and Mars aspects are needed for energy. The more aspects with these two planets, the more active the individual. However, there are varied reactions to Sun and Mars progressed aspects. For example: Some people, if Mars or the Sun is afflicted, have more energy than previously; others, have less. Each person will vary.

If one has major progressed Neptune aspects, a lazy streak may take over. An individual may believe he has sleeping sickness. A Neptune aspect can take physical energy away, if there is nothing to counteract it. If a person has a Mars—Neptune aspect, there is a tendency to be energetic one moment, and tired the next.

* * *

If an individual has *more harmonious aspects* (by major progression) rather than inharmonious ones, there may *not* be enough struggle or desire for accomplishment. It is the discordant aspects which usually drive a person toward success. The favorable aspects tend to make one sit back and wait for everything to be brought in on a gold platter.

* * *

Attracted are those aspects (events) which are needed, for that moment in time. Nothing is ever attracted that can't be handled. People may think, under discordant aspects, that they will never get through a particular situation, but somehow they manage to.

* * *

Astrology is not fatalistic. One has the ability to control the aspects and planets and to make them work in the manner which will be the most beneficial to the individual.

Some examples follow which show how one can gear (guide) the aspect in the direction which will bring the best results. For instance: The 4th house of real estate has favorable major progressed aspects in during a specific time period. Simultaneously, the 5th house of the stock market has unfavorable aspects. With this in mind, the individual should stay out of the stock market and invest in real estate; otherwise, losses can occur.

Another example: The 5th house of love affairs has more harmonious major progressed aspects than the 7th house of marriage (during the same time period).

In a case like this, it is best that the person waits for some favorable 7th house major progressed aspects before leaping into a wedding. However, if the party couldn't wait for more harmonious aspects, then the thinking and attitude toward the spouse and nuptial state should be altered to one of complete harmony. This takes some time to perform, but if the love is important it can be done.

* * *

There are two planets which are difficult to handle in astrology. They are Uranus and Neptune. Actually, a person cannot completely control the events they bring; however, one's reaction to whatever transpires is under the individual's power.

Neptune can be a problem because it brings, as a rule, a disappointment with something one has his heart set on. However, one must think that all is for the best and that the experience attracted was needed for a definite purpose.

Uranus is the planet of surprises. Whenever something shocking happens, the important factor is to handle the event from that point on in a constructive fashion.

For example: If a discordant aspect by major progression is in with Uranus and the 6th or 10th house is involved in the aspect, an individual may quit or be fired from a job.

Either one of these actions should be looked upon in the following manner: Whatever transpires may be the only way possible to have the person leave that job. Maybe there is a better occupation waiting around the corner. It's probable that a complete new line of work may be attracted, which in the long run is more favorable for the individual. Keep in mind that change is progress.

If one will only look back to the past, many years after a discordant major progressed Uranus aspect, a person is most likely to say, "If that hadn't happened to me, I wouldn't be here now doing this. It was a bad incident, the way it occurred, but thank God, it happened!"

Whenever a person dies, the horoscope continues. The individual may be thought or talked about, or receive publicity in some manner. These events can transpire in the future even though the said party is deceased. And the aspects that have continued after death will show the type of publicity received, or how the person is spoken of, or thought about. Look at George Washington and others who still receive publicity and are discussed time and again.

* * *

One can give the trends and the type of energy present in a horoscope. Astrology is a guide, a tool to be utilized in a constructive fashion. And it's all up to the individual which road he wants to crawl, stumble, walk, run, drive or fly down.

* * *

SIGNS OF THE ZODIAC AND SYMBOL   PLANETS AND SYMBOL

♈ Aries	♎ Libra	☉ Sun	♃ Jupiter
♉ Taurus	♏ Scorpio	☽ Moon	♄ Saturn
♊ Gemini	♐ Sagittarius	☿ Mercury	♅ Uranus
♋ Cancer	♑ Capricorn	♀ Venus	♆ Neptune
♌ Leo	♒ Aquarius	♂ Mars	♇ Pluto
♍ Virgo	♓ Pisces		

ASPECTS AND SYMBOL

⊻ Semi-sextile	□ Square
✳ Sextile	☍ Opposition
△ Trine	☌ Conjunction
∠ Semi-square	∥ Parallel
⊡ Sesqui-square	⊼ Inconjunct

CHAPTER ONE

Personal Concerns

Personal Houses in his chart are empty: Nixon tends to place other matters before his personal interests or self.

Virgo rising. Saturn Trine ASC (Virgo rising) and Mercury in Capricorn: His serious countenance, conservativeness in action, dress and opinion are due to the preceeding.

Sun, Mercury and Jupiter in Capricorn and Saturn Square Venus and Square and Parallel the Moon: He tends, at times, to be cold, unemotional and selfish.

Saturn in the 9th house Sextile Neptune in the 11th house, Neptune co-rules the 7th house; Saturn Trine the Sun in the 5th house: Thoughts of security may arise regarding his friends, loved ones, courts, impeachment, travel and foreign relationships.

Mars in the 4th house, co-rules the 3rd house, and is in an Opposition to Pluto in the 10th house:

Danger can be attracted while he is commuting or taking a short distance trip by car, train or bus—or in the home. Accidents, mechanical failures, bombs, explosives, kidnapping, or hijacking can be attracted.

Saturn in the 9th house Sextile Neptune; Saturn Trine Uranus: Journeys can be safer for him by jet rather than those by automobile. The trips by air may be better planned than those on the ground. In the former, some intuition, on his part, may be employed. *NOTE:* Mars and Pluto rule the 3rd house of short distance jaunts and both planets are afflicted.

Mars rules the 8th and co-rules the 3rd house: Nixon is courageous; he does not fear death.

Health

Sun in the 5th house Trine Virgo rising ASC: He is physically strong. His vitality, pep and fortitude can be increased around loved ones, or while in the company of important, famous and wealthy people.

Mercury, Sun and Jupiter in Capricorn; Saturn and Sun Trine the Virgo rising ASC; Pluto Opposition Mars and Mercury: Whenever Nixon is exhausted he has a tendency not to stop, but to push and force himself to continue onward.

Saturn co-rules the 6th house: He may possibly believe that to be sick is a waste of his time.

Pluto in Gemini Opposition Mercury; Mercury rules Virgo—his rising sign, the physical body: His nervous system is one of his weakest areas. When he's under duress, strain or heavy pressure, this nervous condition is visible. The nerves can twitch, his speech is forced with an undercurrent of anger. Every nerve in his body is probably being ordered to obey his command to talk and act normal. Nervous exhaustion may result.

Moon in the 6th house, co-rules the 11th house and is Square and Parallel Saturn in the 9th house; Saturn co-rules the 6th house: His emotions outwardly can be under control. Inwardly, he could suffer with anxiety, worry, fear and a vast concern over an impeachment, lawsuit, court action, foreign negotiation, or how the public will react to these matters.

Trips abroad can be extremely wearing on his emotions. When he arrives home, he could be utterly exhausted.

Jupiter is in a Conjunction and Parallel with Mercury; Mercury rules the Virgo rising ASC— his physical body: Nixon's overeating tends to produce a weight problem and jowls.

Saturn in the 9th house, also co-rules the 5th and 6th house and is Square and Parallel the Moon in the 6th house: There's a tendency for Nixon to have difficulty handling foods which contain dairy products. Constipation can occur with them, or while traveling.

He possibly dislikes to waste food. He may restrict his eating, by staying on a light diet, while on long journeys, or during his stay in foreign countries.

He may eat simple and plain foods when he's on a special regimen, or if he's in the mood for them; however, taste-wise, they probably don't appeal to him.

Moon in the 6th house: Nixon may desire a variety with what he consumes in food.

Jupiter Semi-square Moon and Sextile Venus, in the 6th house: He may enjoy gourmet foods, especially desserts and creamy sauces; however, they aren't that good for his health.

Venus in the 6th house Sextile Mercury and Jupiter in Capricorn: Nixon may take the easy way out, by being diplomatic, when served food which doesn't interest him. He probably doesn't like to hurt the feelings of the host, or to appear unappreciative.

Mental Activities

Virgo rising: He tends to be critical of himself and others. Perfection may be a strong desire of his.

Three planets and the MC are in Air signs in his chart: Most of the time his mind is apt to be up in the air on the mental level of existence.

Virgo rising; Mercury Opposition Pluto in the 10th house; Pluto co-rules the 3rd house; Mars co-rules the 3rd house and is in an Opposition to Pluto and is Inconjunct Saturn in the 9th house; Saturn co-rules the 6th house; Mars is in a Conjunction and Parallel to Mercury: In his early years, an impatience could have been felt with educational institutions because he might have been in a hurry to go to work and accomplish his goals as quickly as possible. However, with his strong determination, patience and force, he could have made himself attend the proper schools.

There's a tendency for Nixon to believe that knowledge is a necessary tool for success. He could feel that with an education he could attain it, and would be able to improve his business, work, position in life, and self.

Virgo rising; Mercury Opposition Pluto in the 10th house; Pluto co-rules the 3rd house: To constantly learn knowledge may be a must with Nixon. He probably is never satisfied with what he knows. With such an active mind, he can be an avid and compulsive reader.

It's possible that if he doesn't read and learn something new, he can't go to sleep at night. Nixon can be similar to a walking encyclopedia—he can share his knowledge by imparting it to others.

* * *

His mental faculties tend to analyze and weigh all factors. He may pay close attention to detail. He tries to make logical deductions. The pros and cons of an issue can make his mind go back and forth as if he's on a mental see-saw. After a lengthy and slow process, the solutions to his problems will probably be discovered. His final decision, on any matter, could seem to take forever.

* * *

To withdraw from crowds, groups and pressures may be a necessity. To be alone, or with his loved ones nearby, so he can do his thinking might possibly be a must. A period of isolation is important, probably because Nixon has to analyze every word that was spoken to him throughout the day.

If he doesn't devote time to this procedure, it's possible that his mind could become, momentarily, cluttered and confused.

Nixon might find that experience is his best teacher; however, he can learn vicariously. Perhaps, listening to the news and rumors, through the media of the radio, television, newspaper, or through individuals, he absorbs what is said with great intensity. He can probably learn through other people's trials and tribulations.

Mercury rules the 1st house and is Semi-sextile Uranus in the 5th house; Uranus co-rules the 6th house; Mercury is in an Opposition to Pluto in the 10th house; Pluto co-rules the 3rd house: When Nixon is relaxed (playing golf, watching sports, or being entertained) unusual ideas from out of left field might pop into his mind. These mental impressions may be unique, original and brilliant. If adopted and cultivated, they can possibly bring favorable changes in business, with the government, or new policies and procedures.

The majority of planets (7) in the third degree of Emanation:
Nixon probably does not always tend to follow his own inner feelings, convictions and desires. His wishes may be altered because he cares about what other people think, suggest and want.

Religion

Saturn in the 9th house:
It's probably difficult for Nixon to express his religious beliefs outwardly. When mentioning the subject, he may appear serious and reserved. To attend church service, he may feel it is his duty.

It's possible that he questions certain portions of the bible, especially if it doesn't make logical sense to him. If this be the case, he could attempt to search for the right answers.

Saturn in the 9th house Sextile Uranus: His mind tends to be open to any "new thought" type of a religion. He may partially break away from his educated beliefs and combine them with a different and modern religion.

Gifts

Sun in the 5th house Semi-square Venus in the 6th house; Venus co-rules the 9th house: Nixon can be the recipient of many expensive and luxurious presents from influential, wealthy and powerful people, at home and abroad. Along these lines, pride may be felt and his ego can be slightly inflated. If the gifts were not his to keep, it could easily disturb him.

* * *

He tends to be a better giver than receiver. If his employees grant him any favors, or work overtime, he will probably be appreciative. This could be shown by his paying them extra money, or giving them a present.

If he gives a gift or bonus and it isn't raved about, he might be hurt and annoyed. However, he's probably too proud to allow anyone to see him react this way; instead, it may wind up as a secret peeve.

4

Socializing

The houses of Life have two planets in them; Saturn co-rules the 5th and 6th house; Venus is in the 6th house: The enjoyment of life can be slightly important to Nixon; however, he can deny himself fun because of his work and all of the responsibilities it entails. Most of the time, his job and social activities are combined as one.

Sun in the 5th house Semi-square Venus in the 6th house: Work possibly rules out his desire to be with those he loves. It might bother him, at times, that he places business before pleasure.

MC Square ASC: His career can create obstacles with his personal activities.

Moon in the 6th house Trine MC and Semi-sextile Sun in the 5th house; the Sun rules the 12th house; Mercury in the 4th house in a Conjunction and Parallel with Jupiter and Opposition Pluto in the 10th house: He may have luck if his family goes along with his public life. When they are a part of it, he can blend possibly his domestic activities with his career. However, it may still remain a conflict when he has to choose between the two. It's probably difficult for him to divide his energies in one area; therefore, his home and business tend to be constantly pulling him in various directions. It's possible that he is proud of the way he handles his constant conflict between the two.

Venus in the 6th house, co-rules the 9th house and is Trine Pluto in the 10th house: Social events can bring favorable television coverage.

Sun in the 5th house, rules the 12th house and is Trine Saturn in the 9th house; Saturn co-rules the 6th house: Secret negotiations can be attended to while entertaining heads of state, influential or wealthy people. The matters discussed can involve silent business deals, or foreign trade.

Nixon probably takes great pride when he's in the company of these important and powerful celebrities. With them good chances for investment can be attracted.

Venus in the 6th house, co-rules the 9th house and is Sextile Jupiter in the 4th house; Jupiter co-rules the 7th house: He may go out of his way to please others. Charm, kindness, cheerfulness and friendliness could be radiated to one and all—that's Nixon. With this in mind, he's probably an excellent host and can greet those he contacts with great warmth.

Three planets and the MC in Air signs and Venus in the 6th house; Venus co-rules the 9th house and is Sextile Mercury which rules the Virgo rising ASC; Mercury is in the 4th house and co-rules the 10th house: At social gatherings, he most likely enjoys learning knowledge. This can be done through his exchanging conversations with others. When this occurs, he may feel that his valuable time is not wasted. Auspicious financial opportunities can be attained when Nixon listens to, and talks with, some of the people he meets at these affairs.

Uranus in the 5th house Semi-sextile Venus in the 6th house; The Moon in Aquarius in the 6th house Semi-sextile Sun in the 5th house:
While he mingles or visits others, he probably notices how they respond to his comments, advice, ideas, offers and recommendations. This method can be employed to test people; later, he may change his plans according to how they reacted—that is, if it proves to his ultimate advantage.

Venus in the 6th house, co-rules the 9th house and is Trine Pluto in the 10th house; Pluto co-rules the 3rd house; Venus is Sextile Mercury; Mercury co-rules the 1st and 10th house and is in the 4th house:
The news media probably will favorably report the social events and banquets given, or attended by, Nixon. If he attends a party, or an affair, which involves the underprivileged or a member of a minority group, good fortune with his career might possibly result.

Venus in the 6th house: Most likely, Nixon will bestow compliments, when deserved, upon his staff. It's possible that, to keep his employees in good spirits, he will invite them to a small party.

Uranus in the 5th house Semi-sextile Venus in the 6th houe and Trine Saturn: A spur of the moment party, or show, may enchant and fascinate him. Unusual, bizarre or way-out entertainment can be gracefully accepted, by Nixon. If originality is shown by the performers, he may find it mentally stimulating. A planned party, or an old-fashioned show can be as equally exciting to him as the unexpected one.

Venus in the 6th house; co-rules the 9th house and is Semi-square Sun in the 5th house; the Sun rules the 12th house; Venus is Square Saturn in the 9th house: Unexpected business can delay Nixon's arrival at a party, or make him cancel it entirely. If the social affair is an important one, he could be disappointed that he is late, or unable to attend.

Sun in Capricorn in the 5th house; the Sun rules the 12th house and is in an Opposition to Neptune in the 11th house: If he held an enormous and spectacular party and some of the invited guests did not come, his ego might be bruised.

* * *

Nixon doesn't like to hurt anyone's feelings, or ego; therefore, if an entertainer disappointed him in the performance of a show, the individual would probably never know it. Most likely, he would handle the person with the utmost diplomacy, and compliment him (or her) in a possible half-truth.

* * *

A pal's conduct could possibly disappoint Nixon, while attending an important and prestigious social event.

Many times, he may withdraw from friends or unimportant and unnecessary social functions, so he can enjoy pleasurable moments with his loved ones.

* * *

Fun

Sun in the 5th house, rules the 12th house and is in an Opposition to Neptune in the 11th house; Sun is Semi-square Venus: Watching movies, television, or going to the theater are possible ways that Nixon can escape from everyday affairs and relax. Most likely, he prefers being surrounded by peace and harmony; however, he may not always have his wishes granted.

Uranus in the 5th house Trine Saturn in the 9th house; Uranus co-rules the 6th house: Games may not hold Nixon's attention because he could consider them a waste of valuable time. However, new ones or a new way to play an old game may fascinate him.

Sports

Mars co-rules the 3rd house and is Inconjunct Saturn which co-rules the 5th house: Sports where there is no risk of bodily harm may interest Nixon.

Mars co-rules the 3rd house and is Semi-sextile Uranus in the 5th house: To *WATCH* dangerous sports could fascinate Nixon.

Sun in the 5th house Opposition Neptune and Semi-square Venus: Golf or fishing, may be enjoyable because with either one of them his mind can forget pressing business, or other, problems. With this relaxed state, the solutions he seeks to any puzzlement can possibly come to light.

Home Life

Three planets in the 4th house: The home tends to be the base for his operations. In it, he can tend to buisness, see people, and enjoy himself with his family. This is an important area of his life.

Mercury and Jupiter in Capricorn in the 4th house: He may resist changes in the home.

A small house, surrounded with only the bare necessities, can be endured momentarily. With hard work, Nixon is likely to change any meager living condition.

Jupiter in the 4th house Sextile Venus: A spacious and expensive home filled with beautiful art treasures or exquisite furnishings may satisfy his desire for beauty and comfort.

Uranus Semi-sextile Mars in the 4th house; Mars co-rules the 3rd house: Nixon might take an interest in the latest gadgets for the home or any new invention involving electronic burglary equipment.

Pluto Opposition Mars, Mercury and Jupiter in the 4th house; Mercury and Jupiter are in Capricorn: His homes may be restrictive, at times, with modern safety devices; however, everyone's well-being comes before anything else. Elaborate alarm systems are possibly required in case of theft or an assassination attempt. Strong police protection with private detectives, or the secret service, will probably be required, or desired.

Pluto Opposition Mercury in the 4th house; Pluto is Semi-sextile and Parallel Saturn; Saturn co-rules the 6th house: Compulsory rules can be enforced in the home, and those living or working there most likely will have to comply.

Mars in Sagittarius in the 4th house Inconjunct Saturn; Mercury in Capricorn in the 4th house Inconjunct Saturn: Freedom to express himself in the home can be important, but with the tight security he is likely to be restrained.

Mercury in Capricorn in the 4th house is in a Conjunction to Jupiter in the 4th house; Mercury rules Virgo rising: Books and papers can be a vital part of his home. Reading and mental activities will probably make up the major part of his life.

At times, he may feel weighed down with his many responsibilities, but he will probably pull out of that mood with a happy-go-lucky one.

Jupiter in the 4th house Sextile Venus: Affection, pleasant feelings and contentedness is probably felt in the home with his loved ones. Nixon, most likely, prefers people to laugh, be merry and have fun. While in this state of mind, he can be an extrovert and optimist—confidence seems to reign.

Mercury in the 4th house Semi-sextile Uranus in the 5th house: Conversations, in the home, with an exchange of intellect and wit, can stimulate Nixon's mind. People who express unusual and different views can fascinate him. Possibly, many of his good ideas stem from these chit-chats.

Mercury in the 4th house Opposition Pluto in the 10th house: The words spoken in the home environment can reach the public's ears through the press, television, radio, transcripts, or tapes.

Mars in the 4th house; Mercury in the 4th house Sextile Venus: Impatience with self and others can be a problem with those who are around him. His temper is possibly more noticeable in the place where he resides rather than when he is out of the home environment. Strife is easily attracted in the home atmosphere. However, a loved one can calm him down with endearing words.

8

Mars in the 4th house, co-rules the 3rd house and rules the 8th house and is in an Opposition to Pluto in the 10th house: Groups of people with banners outside the doors of a residence of his might antagonize and anger him. Sit-down-strikes, fire and violence can be attracted.

Nixon tends to be brave and may possibly dare anyone to cause him a problem. Assassination can occur in the home, or the surroundings—like the gardens, or outdoors.

NOTE: Mars and Pluto are the two planets involved in an assassination. This does *not* imply that it will happen to him, but under this aspect, it can be attracted; however, he may utilize the energy in another manner.

Court

Saturn in the 9th house: Nixon tends to take legal matters seriously. Just thinking about a lawsuit might make him react with anxieties, apprehensions and worries.

Saturn in the 9th house Trine the Sun which rules the 12th house; Saturn Trine Uranus: Any court case is likely to be carefully planned by Nixon. He tends to be cautious, shrewd, evasive and is a good, natural psychologist. If he uses the proper strategy it can be to his advantage.

Saturn in the 9th house and co-rules 6th house: Nixon can cleverly maneuver delays with court cases. He could probably discover ways and means to avoid an appearance in front of a judge or jury.

If he has a legal matter pending, rather than spending time worrying about it, he probably adds on more work and responsibility.

Saturn in the 9th house Square Venus in the 6th house: He psychically could feel that he should not confide in all of the members of his staff, or employees. It might possibly worry Nixon that an aide, or the help, would testify against him in court.

Saturn in the 9th house Square Moon in the 6th house; Venus in the 6th house Semi-square Sun which rules the 12th house: If a member of his staff, ex-aide or subordinate testified against him in court, Nixon would probably be hurt emotionally; however, his sensitiveness would likely to be hidden and outwardly he could appear indifferent.

Saturn in the 9th house Square and Parallel Moon in the 6th house: If he lost a legal case, the defeat may appear to the public and those who have worked under him, as an open admission to guilt—to Nixon it would be a disaster.

CHAPTER TWO

Close Relationships

Affection, love and sex

Seven planets in the Companionship houses: The company of loved ones are enjoyed by Nixon. It would be almost impossible for him to live alone. Constantly having loved ones nearby is a must.

Moon in the 6th house Semi-sextile Sun in the 5th house; Venus in Pisces in the 6th house Sextile Jupiter; Jupiter is in the 4th house, co-rules the 7th house: He tends to be warm and affectionate with the people, and animals, he loves. To protect and take care of them may be his desire. Most likely, he enjoys administering to their needs and wants. Nixon can be extremely compassionate and kind.

Venus in the 6th house Semi-square Sun in the 5th house: A pat on the back for a job well done could be desired from those he's fond of. He probably adores their approval, praise and compliments; without it, his ego might be hurt.

Uranus in the 5th house Semi-sextile Venus and Mars: His views on sex can be different, unusual or unconventional.

Sun in the 5th house, in Capricorn, Trine Saturn: With sex he has a tendency to be prudish, proper and moral; especially, if he respects the person.

Moderation with sex could be used.

Venus Sextile Mars: Nixon can blend, harmoniously, his strong love nature with his physical sexual needs.

Sun in the 5th house: Great pride may be felt for his virility and sexual power.

Mars co-rules the 3rd house and is in the 4th house in a Conjunction to Jupiter in the 4th house: Nixon may desire, and can have, an abundance of sex.

Venus Sextile Mars and Square Saturn; Saturn co-rules the 5th house: He has no sex problem. At times, he may feel it is a duty, but once aroused, his attitude probably changes.

He can be physically sexy; however, there are times when he has trouble expressing and showing his most delicate and tender love feelings. There tends to be an emotional part of him that's not given completely to the one he loves.

Perhaps, he yearns to let go and not restrain himself, but something seems to hold him back. The cause of the repression could be a defense mechanism, fear of loving too deeply, getting hurt, losing the loved one, or puritanical thoughts.

Marriage

Neptune co-rules the 7th house: Nixon tends to have an ideal in mind for a mate. Once found, she is probably placed on a pedestal.

Uranus in the 5th house Sextile Venus and Semi-sextile Jupiter and Parallel Neptune; Jupiter and Neptune co-rule the 7th house: With his wife, he can be enchanted, fascinated, magnetized and swept off his feet.

Sun in the 5th house, rules the 12th house, and is in an Opposition to Neptune in the 11th house; Neptune co-rules the 7th house: Castle-building fantasies can take place if he gives Pat imaginary attributes which don't exist. Upon awakening to reality, there's a possibility of his being disillusioned or disappointed in her.

* * *

If acquaintances, friends, or men in official, dignified or eminent positions were to cheat on their spouses, Nixon would most likely be disappointed in those people's conduct and behavior. It's possible that this action would make him change his feelings toward those individuals, and could impair their relationship.

If Nixon knew that a particular person was having an extracurricular love affair, he probably would not become involved with that person in a conversation that led in that direction.

Jupiter co-rules the 7th house and is in a Conjunction and Parallel with Mercury and is Sextile Venus and Semi-sextile Uranus and Parallel the MC: Nixon will probably rely upon his wife's aid and support in every direction possible.

Jupiter co-rules the 7th house and is in a Conjunction and Parallel with Mercury in the 4th house: To communicate with Patricia is, perhaps, a necessity. They can exchange ideas, share knowledge, discuss his work and she can inspire him. These, most likely, are the pleasures he enjoys. He attracts a mate who tends to have faith and confidence in him. It's possible that she can encourage him in business and other areas.

Neptune co-rules the 7th house and is Sextile Saturn which co-rules the 5th house: When he's down in the dumps, Pat can probably cheer him up. When he's with her, he tends to laugh and be happy.

12

Sun in the 5th house Trine Saturn; Saturn co-rules the 5th house: There's a tendency for him to try everything possible to make his marriage work. A solid and lasting relationship is a must. Nixon is most likely very proud of Pat. She tends to have his respect.

Venus in Pisces: He tends to be slightly servile to his mate.

Venus in Pisces Sextile Mercury, Mars and Jupiter and Trine Pluto: With his wife he can be steady, reliable, pliable, giving, receptive, grateful, forgiving, cooperative, fiery, happy, spiritual, religious, and romantic. He may feel beautiful thoughts of love for her. He tends to be extremely and intensely affectionate. He is warm and sensitive and tends to cling to his loved ones.

Uranus in the 5th house Semi-sextile Jupiter and Venus and Parallel Neptune; Jupiter and Neptune co-rule the 7th house: Possibly, when his mate gives him freedom and independence to work and she doesn't nag him, he will probably love her all the more.

Saturn co-rules the 5th house and is Sextile Neptune; Neptune co-rules the 7th house; Saturn is Square Venus; Venus rules the 2nd and 6th house: He tends to desire security for Pat and will probably work hard to give it to her. There are occasions when he might feel guilty because business and his ambitions interfere in their relationship.

Saturn co-rules the 5th house and is Sextile Neptune; Neptune co-rules the 7th house; Saturn is Square Venus; Venus is in the 6th house and co-rules the 9th house: His trips or campaigns can keep Pat and him apart. Most of the time, he will probably prefer her to travel with him. If she isn't with him, he could miss her.

Mars in the 4th house in a Conjunction and Parallel to Jupiter in the 4th house; Jupiter co-rules the 7th house: If Pat moves too slowly, his impatience with her is likely to show. Tempermental outbreaks can occur when they disagree about business or his brothers. Quarrels may take place over the too free spending of money (on his part), or about his loans, debts, taxes or real estate transactions. He tends to hurt her feelings when he speaks impulsively. Nixon doesn't like to upset anyone, especially his wife.

Venus in Pisces Sextile Jupiter; Jupiter co-rules the 7th house: He has to be careful that he doesn't take Pat for granted. Nixon needs a wife who is friendly, kind, sweet and a good mixer at social functions.

Sun in the 5th house, rules the 12th house and is Semi-square Venus and Opposition Neptune; Neptune co-rules the 7th house: A secret desire of Nixon's may be to hide away from his friends and be with Patricia.

* * *

His ego can be hurt by a loved one, especially, if she turns him down, or doesn't give him enough attention. Any annoyances and irritations which he possibly may feel, he will tend to keep to himself.

Saturn is in the 9th house and co-rules the 5th house and is Sextile Neptune; Neptune co-rules the 7th house: To be unfaithful to his marriage partner is likely to be against his puritanical and religious outlook, or moral code.

Children

Nixon can admire, respect and be proud of his daughters; he can receive the same from them.

Uranus in the 5th house Semi-sextile Venus and Trine Saturn; Sun in the 5th house Parallel MC and Opposition Neptune in the 11th house; Neptune co-rules the 7th house: Favors received from his daughters might make him glow. They can depend upon him. He, most likely, relies upon their confidence, help and love.

If his children aid his career (like campaigning), or help his reputation (like defending him), he will probably glow with great pride. Any publicity received in behalf of them can possibly benefit his image or job. If a daughter wins an award, honor or diploma, he will probably brag about it to his friends and acquaintances.

Uranus in the 5th house and Saturn co-rules it: Nixon tends to give a certain amount of freedom and independence to his daughters; however, he can be strict. He is likely to be concerned deeply about their welfare. Giving them security may be part of a plan he could have for their future.

Sun in 5th house, rules 12th house, and is Semi-square Venus in the 6th house: When his work interferes with their having a good time, the daughters probably understand; however, Nixon, might be extremely sensitive in this area. It may annoy him, that he can't spend more moments with them. If they ever said anything to him against his work, he'd be hurt. They could easily knock his ego down.

He might be secretly disappointed in a daughter who was lazy, too pliable and soft. There are times when it could be difficult for him to say "no" when asked for money, or a favor, from any offspring. He probably dislikes refusing his loved ones anything.

Sun in the 5th house, rules the 12th house and is in an Opposition to Neptune: Upsets to his ego can possibly occur if his daughters tell him a fib. Any exaggerations made by them can bring a disillusionment—he won't believe they can lie. However, if they caught him in a fabrication, it could bother him to no end.

Nixon can break a promise regarding a vacation, outing, theater, or recreational activity because of his business. When this happens everyone involved can be disappointed.

Uranus in the 5th house, co-rules 6th house: If his offspring interest him in something new, different, intriguing or fascinating, he may be mentally

14

stimulated by it. Through them he might possibly adopt new and modern ways of thinking and acting.

Uranus in the 5th house Semi-sextile Venus and Trine Saturn: Entertainment or a surprise party for his children can give him great pleasure. If they do the same for him, he will have a favorable response. Gifts that are given and received could be unique and practical.

Sun in the 5th house, in Capricorn, Trine Saturn in the 9th house: His ideal for a son-in-law is some whom he can respect and admire. Nixon tends to be particular who a daughter of his marries. A lasting relationshp is probably what he desires for her. To please him, the son-in-law should, perhaps, be conservative, practical, serious and ambitious.

Brothers

Pluto co-rules the 3rd house and is in the 10th house in an Opposition to Jupiter in the 4th house; Jupiter co-rules the 7th house: Happy times can be had with his brothers. He tends to be overconfident and optimistic with their business plans, which may include a partnership with him. When Nixon feels they are doing well, his mood with them may be one of laughter and having fun; however, he can turn the opposite direction and become a tyrant. He may try to run their lives, or careers.

Mars in the 4th house in a Conjunction and Parallel to Mercury and Jupiter in the 4th house; Mars co-rules the 3rd house: With, or about his brothers, he can cuss, be hasty, make snap judgments and later, perhaps, turn the other cheek and say he doesn't care what they do. If they don't use their intellect this could burn him up—he likes intelligent people.

Pluto co-rules the 3rd house and is in the 10th house in an Opposition to Mars and Mercury in the 4th house: His brothers can cost him plenty, or help keep him in debt and hot water. Nixon could easily loan them enormous amounts of money, or they could possibly use his name and acquire a bank loan. The funds may go toward real estate investment. It's possible that Nixon feels he must help them in any way that he can—it's as if he was compelled to assist them.

* * *

There are times when Nixon could be torn back and forth in a terrific conflict about his brothers. He may wonder whether he should loan them money, co-sign a note, go into a partnership with them, or become involved in a real estate transaction.

15

* * *

It's possible that he will encourage, or push them into a business. Nixon may dictate to them certain rules which should be followed; if broken, all hell can break loose.

He could make drastic changes on their behalf. Whatever action is taken, he probably believes that it is for everyone's best interest.

* * *

If Nixon speaks too hastily, misunderstandings can easily occur with his brothers. His impatience with them may lead to strife. The home environment, on short distance trips, commuting, on the telephone, intercom, and with correspondence—these are the areas where Nixon's temper can be easily shown with his brothers.

* * *

Arguments and tension may be out in the open between the brothers and the press, or Nixon and the reporters.

It's possible that Nixon will clue his brothers in on what they should say when interviewed by the news media. Nixon and his brothers can be misquoted by the press.

* * *

Political parties, or people who represent them, may try to use persuasive methods to make Nixon do as they command. He will probably rebel. To save his brothers and himself from ruin, Nixon might do something that is against his desires and principles.

* * *

His anger can be aroused if a legal case (with his brothers) lingers, is delayed, or hashed over time and again. Nixon's impatience for everything to blow over and be forgotten can be noticed by everyone.

* * *

Nixon should take extra caution with himself and his brothers regarding possible frame-ups, extortions, or kidnappings. Perhaps, added police protection will be a necessity. Bad publicity can result.

16

Mars co-rules the 3rd house and rules the 8th house and is in the 4th house in an Inconjunct to Saturn in the 9th house: Anxieties may arise if Nixon had to go to court because of his brothers, or if they had to appear because of something they did, especially, if other people's money was involved in any misdeed. Doubts and uncertainties, in this direction, can prey constantly on Nixon's mind.

* * *

Many times, when his temper starts to rise, he may say, "What's the use? What good will it do to tell him (a brother) what I really think?"

After some reflection, along these lines, Nixon may decide to remain silent on all issues.

Pluto co-rules the 3rd house and is in the 10th house in an Opposition to Jupiter, Mars and Mercury in the 4th house: If Nixon leaps, without thinking, into a business relationship with his brothers, he can possibly attract bad publicity, scandals and many other harassing problems. In trying to benefit them, the role of the fall guy may be his.

Friends and Acquaintances

One planet in an Association house: To associate daily with people, for social purposes only, is not likely to be a favorite pastime of Richard Nixon's.

Neptune in the 11th house in Cancer: Nixon can be emotional and sensitive with his comrades, but does not tend to show these feelings. Instead, he may retreat to a crab-like shell of protective covering and appear cool. Perhaps, by being this way, he feels he can't be hurt by anyone.

* * *

The type of buddies and acquaintances Nixon can attract are promoters, idealists, poets, playboys, movie stars, theatrical personalities, or those from the field of aviation.

Moon in the 6th house, co-rules the 11th house: The common class from all walks of life, the public, or employees are the other types of people he can attact for friends and acquaintances.

Neptune in the 11th house Parallel Uranus in the 5th house; Uranus co-rules the 6th house: Those who are eccentric, unusual, unconventional, or inventors may also be attracted for pals, or acquaintances. Fascinating stories can be told by these friends who dare to do the impossible, something new or different. Nixon can be held spellbound by them. Enthralled, perhaps, by what they relate, he could be mentally stimulated by their conversations.

Through their unique views, he can become involved in out of the ordinary enterprises. With these people, he probably never knows what to expect next. They can pop in and out of his life periodically.

* * *

Disruptions of his plans and cancellations with entertainment can strike like lightning from out of the clear blue sky. Freedom and independence, perhaps, is needed with his friends so he can tend to his business any time an emergency arises.

Neptune in the 11th house Sextile Saturn: Older, sedate, conservative and serious friends and acquaintances can also be attracted into Nixon's life.

It's likely that his past disappointments, with so-called pals, are partly responsible for his distrust of people. Diplomacy may be used with those he meets. He tends to be cautious and might possibly make slow, rather than quick, friendships.

When he follows this system he may discover that he has a better chance to attract lasting and solid relationships. Once he figures he can count on and trust a person, he could feel secure with that individual and probably enjoys holding on to that friendship.

Most likely, this type of pal can depend on Nixon and he will possibly be as loyal to them as they are to him. These buddies could, perhaps, come to his aid in case of an impeachment, or court action.

* * *

When he travels on a long distance trip, or to a foreign country, deep and earnest individuals may become his friends. Nixon can use them and they, in turn, might take advantage of him. His feelings, along these lines, are probably that this is a fair exchange. These people can be to Nixon's benefit in international trade, with real estate transactions, or any form of a negotiation.

* * *

He may tell his close chums of his idealistic views for the world. These buddies, if they agree, could possibly give him suggestions to help make this universe a better place for everyone.

Moon in the 6th house, co-rules the 11th house, and is Trine and Parallel Pluto in the 10th house: The close cooperation of his acquaintances and friends (who work beneath him in position) can be gained. Nixon possibly desires to protect them from harm and to take care of them. Perhaps, it's because they tend to go along with his plans, or it's possible that Nixon feels paternal toward them.

Neptune in the 11th house, co-rules the 7th house, and is in an Opposition to the Sun in the 5th house; the Sun rules the 12th house: Fabricators and people with power or in authoritative positions such as politicians, ambassadors, heads of state, royalty, wealthy, eminent or famous—these individuals may become friends or acquaintances.

* * *

Friends and loved ones can create conflicts. Nixon may enjoy being with both; however, he can't give them all his undivided attention at the same time; thus, he could keep them separated.

Business deals with his companions may be kept as secretive as his personal affairs which, also, may involve them.

* * *

Nixon can brag to his companions, or they may boast to him. Of course, he may not believe in all that they say, but it may sound good.

* * *

A playboy, or lazy type who hasn't accomplished much, can possibly disturb Nixon; therefore, he may not desire to be in the person's presence. If an individual in this category asked him to a social gathering, it's possible that he would have an alibi and decline the invitation.

Nixon tends to admire, respect, idolize and look up to those who have mastered great feats or tasks, earned fame or money. These acquaintances, or cronies, may be movie stars, royalty, heads of state, or anyone in a powerful, or top position. However, once he becomes close to them, he may be shattered if they don't measure up to his expectations.

* * *

Nixon is inclined to confide in and place too much reliance on some of his friends. Some may attempt to solicitate his sympathy and pity. If they have suffered, he is susceptible to being influenced by them because he probably feels sorry for them. He tends to be too compassionate toward their problems.

* * *

Nixon's misplaced confidence can possibly attract his destruction. Later, he may regret that he trusted and believed in a person.

Sorrows and disappointments can be in store for Nixon when he discovers that a pal is later a foe.

His real enemies may be those he relied upon and didn't suspect, such as those acquaintances, or buddies who are politicians, executives, staff members or have affluence. Also, anyone who tries to block his constructive efforts or hold him back in business can later turn out to be an adversary.

* * *

Some of his friends may possibly concoct schemes for overnight riches. If Nixon is conned into becoming involved, the following can result: Misrepresentation, fraud, cheating, deception, lies, broken promises or unrealized hopes. Any criminal activity involving a trusted pal, or someone in a high office, can be upsetting news to Nixon.

Companions who pull any of the preceding will probably hurt his pride and ego. With these transactions, deals with most likely fall through at the last minute. Because of them, Nixon can be out on a limb. When the branch breaks, he will possibly be made the fall guy. The whole mess can be dumped into his lap.

He probably doesn't want others to know the truth of how he was misled or fooled; therefore, he may cover for them by keeping everything confidential.

* * *

Nixon tends to be a smooth talker with gentle persuasive methods (when he uses them). As a result, companions may violate a trust with another or break a rule so they can help him. They may even falsify papers, documents or deeds.

His friends may lie for him or he may fabricate, cover up and camouflage their mistakes. Nixon may show a false front to hide any wrong doings. Some of these companions may abandon him in a crisis, or it's possible that he may leave others to take the blame.

Neptune in the 11th house Sextile Saturn in the 9th house; Saturn Trine Sun: Wealthy and influential friends can come to his aid, at the last moment, and save him. They may, in court, take the rap for him. Nixon tends to have extremely strong and compassionate feelings for these dear buddies.

CHAPTER THREE

Work

ASC Slow (ASC moves slower than MC-rising sign moves slower than career angle.): Many opportunities could have been presented to Nixon in his early youth; however, he might not have been able to seize them all.

With something important, most likely, Nixon will not bluff. Perhaps, he feels that if he doesn't have confidence in a situation or business, he prefers to wait until he does.

Saturn Retrograde (Rx) in his natal-birth chart: It's possible that in his earlier years he was unable to make long range business plans.

Saturn Turned Direct in motion in his progressed chart: Most likely, in his later years he has been able to plan ahead and stick with his carefully laid plots.

Sun in Capricorn in the 5th house Parallel MC: Nixon desires approval and acceptance from others. To receive it, he can direct his thoughts in a planned direction and remain firm.

The majority of the planets are on the West, right-hand side of chart: Through the help of others, Nixon tends to rise to a high position. To do it solely on his own can be too difficult. He probably needs to be surrounded by an entourage of people who work for, wait upon and give him valuable information.

Perhaps, this reliance upon others can make him somewhat under their control. This could disturb him because he might want complete power. He most likely feels that he has no choice other than to accept conditions, situations, environment, changes and people. These actions, on his part, can possibly make him a victim of circumstances.

Three planets in fixed signs: Nixon can be stubborn. There's a tendency for him to be unyielding with his ideas and opinions. He seems to know his own mind.

Once he makes a decision on a particular subject, he probably won't budge. He tends to be solid as a rock, set in his ways and may resist change. If he has to swerve from his plans, it might bother him.

Possibly, he will sit and stew for awhile. But that will not likely last for long. Nixon tends to feel determined to succeed in spite of all obstacles. To resign or to accept defeat—these can be foreign words to Nixon's ears. However, if he

21

ever goes in this direction, it's possible that there is no other way out. In this case, if it's to his advantage, he will probably take this route as a very last resort.

Four planets in Cardinal signs: Action and keeping busy may possibly be desired, because stagnation probably is not his cup of tea. Nixon tends to be a pioneer and can start new areas for development.

Three planets in Fixed signs and three planets in Capricorn and Saturn a co-rule of the 6th: Whatever he initiates he will, most likely, do his best for it's completion.

Four planets and ASC in Earth signs and Saturn co-rules the 6th house: To toil and work hard for material gains can be extremely important.

Pluto in Gemini in the 10th house and three planets in Capricorn and Saturn co-rules the 6th house and Four planets in Energy houses: If necessary, Nixon can perform a job without ever taking any time off—he could work eighteen hours a day, for seven days a week, without ever taking a rest or vacation. His stamina tends to be that dynamic.

Four planets in energy houses, Sun Trine ASC (Virgo rising): If Nixon doesn't have an outlet for his abundant vitality, he tends to become mentally restless.

Three planets in Fixed signs; Virgo rising; Mercury in Capricorn; Saturn co-rules the 6th house and is in the 9th house in a Trine to the Sun in Capricorn and the Virgo rising ASC: Efficiency is probably a must for him. Nixon tends to be a perfectionist. His attention can easily be concentrated in one direction. Most likely, details won't be missed. He can obtain the facts and examine them by placing them in their proper perspective. Shrewdness may be part of his makeup.

Mars co-rules the 3rd house and is an Inconjunct to Saturn; Saturn co-rules the 6th house and Mars is in an Opposition to Pluto in the 10th house and is in a Conjunction and Parallel with Mercury in the 4th house; Mercury rules the Virgo rising—the 1st house: There probably aren't many spare moments for him to call his own. He could feel that he will never catch up with all of the work he has outlined to do. Possibly, if he falls behind, he might plunge in to make up for lost time.

Saturn co-rules 6th house: The constant use of his time is probably a necessity. To waste it may be an annoyance. He tends to thrive by living on a tight schedule with deadlines to meet and working under enormous pressure.

His self-discipline is quite remarkable. He can perform, for hours on end, monotonous, tedious and routine work. He will probably stick persistently to a job until it's completed.

Nixon can gripe if he has too much, and complain if he has too little to do. With a lack of work, he may panic. To avoid this, he probably will add burdens and responsibilities to his schedule. He tends to work harder when he knows he has to accomplish everything on the agenda.

* * *

Once Nixon trusts someone who works for him, he probably prefers to keep the person in his employ for as long as possible.

Moon and Venus in the 6th house: Variety could be needed with his job; otherwise, a temporary restlessness or boredom is likely to set in. Whenever his routine is disrupted, or plans changed, it's possible that he will adapt by taking the easy way out.

Venus in Pisces in the 6th house Semi-square Sun in the 5th house and Semi-sextile Uranus in the 5th house: It's possible that, while he's laboring over some dilemma, a lazy streak will take over. When this occurs, he may follow the line of least resistance and allow his mind to wander to pleasurable areas. By doing this, the answer to a problem is likely to pop into his mind.

Mars in the 4th house in a Conjunction and Parallel to Mercury: His correspondence may be attended to as fast as possible. Once he has made a decision to sign a paper, he probably does it hurriedly.

Mars co-rules the 3rd house: To talk on the telephone, he may feel is a nuisance, if there are other more important pending matters. There's a tendency for him to be impatient and speak fast. His temper is likely to be easily aroused while conversing on the phone.

* * *

The fastest transportation available suits him fine because he could dislike wasting his time traveling. If he isn't working while being chauffered, he may fidget because he's in a hurry to reach his distination.

Three planets and the MC and ASC in Adapatable signs: If necessary, Nixon can adjust to quick changes. His easiest areas for adaptability may be: Any matter which may damage his reputation, job, business, employees, real estate, brothers, home or diet.

Venus in Pisces in the 6th house: With his employees he tends to be emotional, sensitive, kind, gracious and charming.

Moon in Aquarius in the 6th house: Psychology and intuition can be used with his aides or the help. He may take them under his wing and take an interest in their affairs and problems. It's possible that he will try to understand their likes and dislikes.

As a public servant, he probably enjoys catering to the common populace. To give them good service could be uppermost in his mind. He tends to be a humanitarian along these lines.

23

Jupiter co-rules the 7th house and is Semi-square the Moon in the 6th house: With the public, he tends to maintain an attitude that all is going well. His conception may be that all problems will be taken care of eventually. His overconfidence and assurance is what the public sees.

He may desire to give hope and reassurance to his employees. It could be overdone, or he may feel too confident with them. If it backfires, he might become slightly peeved.

He tends to be less liked by the general populace whenever he makes unwise aims, moves or changes. If he takes the people for granted or is too sure that they will go for his exaggerated plans, possibly he will feel annoyed with the way they react.

Uranus in the 5th house, co-rules the 6th house; Venus is in the 6th house and is Semi-sextile Uranus: The work schedule for his staff can possibly be turned upside-down with constant emergencies. Nixon may desire to have the latest in office machinery for his employees. The cost of said equipment probably is unimportant—it's likely to be the speed which can be attained that could be uppermost in Nixon's mind. Short-cut methods to work can possibly appeal to him.

Venus in the 6th house Semi-square Sun in the 5th house: If an employee makes an error, it's possible that Nixon will become provoked with the person. Because he probably doesn't like to hurt anyone's feelings, there's a tendency for him to find the easiest way possible to handle the mistake made.

Three planets in Fixed signs and Saturn in Taurus in the 9th house Semi-sextile and Parallel Pluto, Inconjunct Mercury, Square and Parallel Moon and Venus and Trine Sun in Capricorn in the 5th house: To let go of people, a job, papers, transcripts or tapes could be something Nixon detests. His main stubbornness, in these areas, are possibly with employees, foreigners, loved ones, judges, court actions; verdicts; other nations; religion, entertaining; diet; work and all risks including the stock market.

Saturn in the 9th house, co-rules the 6th house and is Square and Parallel Moon in the 6th house: He could fear losing his job through an impeachment or illness. This might bother him because he would be powerless to help the poverty-stricken in foreign lands. He tends to have a desire to be needed; if it's taken away, despondent moods may strike. Possibly, this is one of his motives for delaying court actions, keeping silent about any sickness and remaining quiet about his aides (ex, or present), and holding on to his work for as long as possible.

He may desire to notify people of the latest events; however, it's likely that everything is not reported. This might be due to the fact that he doesn't want people to be panic-stricken or in fear because of something he may state to them.

24

Saturn in the 9th house Square and Parallel the Moon in Aquarius in the 6th house; Saturn Trine Uranus; Uranus co-rules the 6th house: Nixon, most likely, has all of his speeches to the public scrutinized in advance by his staff, or employees. He may employ strategy and psychology with the words he speaks.

Saturn in the 9th house Square and Parallel the Moon in the 6th house and a Lack of Fire Signs in his chart: His speeches from the public platform, including radio and television, tend to be serious with a lack of enthusiasm. This can also create difficulty with his inspiring others to become interested in his project and plans.

Saturn in the 9th house Square Venus and Square and Parallel the Moon in the 6th house: Unpopularity can occur with the general public when Nixon enforces strict rules, regulations, laws and eliminates waste, cuts down on the costs and budgets, rolls back the prices, enacts a freeze on wages or goods.

With these actions, people may react with fright. It could make them hold on to their money because possibly they feel a depression is either on, or coming.

Perhaps, Nixon instinctively knows that everyone will not agree with his conservative issues or plans. However, he probably believes that he is taking the right and proper action. Outwardly, he may react somber, determined and grim. Inwardly, Nixon can be hurt, sensitive, depressed, worried and quite negative.

Sun in the 5th house Trine ASC; The ASC rules his 1st house and is Trine Saturn—Saturn rules the 9th house and co-rules the 6th house: His greatest pride may be in dealing with heads of state, ambassadors, royalty, influential and wealthy people, or those who are celebrities and have left their imprint upon the world. These individuals tend to give him pep, energy and raise his vitality when he's in their company. He may be comfortable in the presence of important people, and he probably feels that he can handle them with the dignity they deserve.

Moon in Aquarius in the 6th house; Uranus in Aquarius co-rules the 6th house and is Semi-sextile Mercury in the 4th house—Mercury rules the ASC, his personality: To read human nature is probably easy for Nixon to do. It's possible that when he talks to another, the facial reactions to his words are observed. If the said party does not agree with him, he might change his words so the individual will go along with his ideas.

Moon in Aquarius in the 6th house Trine Pluto in the 10th house: Nixon tends to be intuitive. His role to help serve the populace may be aided, if he learns the likes and dislikes of people from all walks of life. By placing himself in their position and taking action on their behalf, the result, most likely, will prove to be extremely lucky for all concerned.

Pluto in the 10th house Trine and Parallel the Moon in the 6th house and Semi-sextile and Parallel Saturn in the 9th house: It's possible that his ambitious nature is combined with a desire to do good deeds for humanity. To help a large and deserving group, or a cause that brings betterment for all people, is perhaps in his upper most mind. He tends to have an intense interest to aid and assist the poor or underprivileged.

The public is likely to respond favorably when he appears on television with his ideas on humanitarian causes. When he abides by that which is preached, it's possible that he will gain their cooperation and assistance.

Venus in the 6th house Trine Pluto in the 10th house: Nixon can be kind, compassionate and understanding when it serves his purpose.

Pluto in the 10th house Trine and Parallel the Moon in the 6th house: The general populace might respect him whenever he advances deserving and meritorious causes for the good of society. If he discusses world peace ideas, on television, or the radio, the public could respond favorably to him.

Investigations he or others make regarding his staff, employees or job is likely to bring drastic changes in the government. If anything is exposed, Nixon's best bet is to appear on television and radio and appeal to the public by being emotional, warm, soft-spoken and compassionate. In this manner, he is likely to gain the sympathy and cheers he craves.

Saturn in the 9th house and co-rules the 6th house is Trine Uranus; Uranus co-rules the 6th house: Modern and new techniques which involve business, the government and foreign nations, or trade, can be advantageous for Nixon. Luck can result when he blends his conservative nature with new thought and liberal actions.

Good fortune, or results, can come flying in whenever Nixon has old laws changed, revised, amended or brought up-to-date. His unusual ideas which could possibly involve the liberty of others, or new policies, could probably prove to be to his benefit.

The Sun rules the 12th house and is Trine Saturn in the 9th house and Semi-sextile the Moon in the 6th house: The public is probably told what Nixon wishes them to know. Any confidential matter he can keep secret.

Three planets in Psychic houses: Mystery, intrigue, secrecy, the unknown and, perhaps, the occult (including astrology) can appeal to Nixon.

Jupiter co-rules the 7th house and is Parallel MC (the 10th house cusp): It's possible that Nixon has a step-by-step outline planned regarding an idea for peace among all nations. Most likely, this projects fruition could be gradual rather than being an overnight affair. If publicity is received, along these lines, it might be slow in coming; but it can possibly build to great heights. This could give Nixon a contented and happing feeling.

Sun in the 5th house and rules the 12th house and is in an Opposition to Neptune in the 11th house; Neptune co-rules the 7th house: Perhaps, his most secretive areas that he probably doesn't want people to know about are: The gambles and chances he takes in life, including the stock market; secret negotiations with heads of state, politicians, leaders of industry, or those of affluence; his friends and loved ones; entertaining; fun; sex.

On many occasions, Nixon might make a public vow, pledge his word of honor, guarantee or commit himself to a plan, project or undertaking, and only ten percent of what is promised, or agreed upon, may result.

The commitments or contracts which are possibly made by him, or others, may not be performed; but it is not always his fault. Consequently, he will probably be blamed for talking big and not fulfilling his part in the enterprise.

* * *

There's a tendency for him to stretch a point, play possum and answer questions vaguely. Information may possibly be withheld, or a half-truth may be told by Nixon. Records and documents are likely to be falsified by his friends or enemies, at Richard's request, or secretively, without his knowing it. Whatever takes place, he will probably receive the blame. Actuality, as a result, can be twisted and warped.

Pluto in Gemini in the 10th house: More than one occupation at a time can be handled.

Nixon can possibly make compulsory rules for others to follow. He tends to be ruthless. He could feel that force is the only means to gain his way. To do so, pressure may be brought to bear upon others. His main problem is dictativeness.

Pluto in the 10th house, co-rules the 3rd house and is in an Opposition to Mercury in Capricorn in the 4th house: Perhaps, no interference will be too great for him to conquer. Most likely, he will not allow anyone to stand in his pathway. To gain his end result, he may employ all types of ways and means. People may be used to further his aims.

Mercury and Jupiter in Capricorn in the 4th house in an Opposition to Pluto in the 10th house: Ambitious, Nixon appears to be driven with an obsession to reach the pinnacle of success. Similar to the mountain goat, he may feel that a climb to the top of the mountain is a must.

He can advance slowly, in spite of all hurdles. Nixon will most likely always look ahead, never down or back. A fall means that he will probably rise again. There's a tendency to continue upward and to never give up until his goals are accomplished. Nixon's persistent aim, perhaps, is toward the greatest heights attainable—the top of the ladder.

Jupiter co-rules the 7th house is in an Opposition to Pluto in 10th house: Nixon tends to be overconfident with his control over others. He might possibly aim too high and overshoot his mark. He may tell the public that everything is going great guns. The words can be spoken with a tremendous force. Most likely, he believes in his optimistic statements.

Pluto in the 10th house Opposition Mercury which also rules his ASC-personality: His forcefulness, or tendency to omit facts, can create many difficulties when he tells his ideas to groups of people. This includes minorities, those who have causes, political parties or any body of people such as a committee, commission or labor union.

Pluto in Gemini Opposition Mercury, Mars and Jupiter in Capricorn: It's possible that whenever his staff erases, edits or types any transcript, document, or tape, Nixon can neglect to catch the mistakes or omissions made. These blunders may be done intentionally, or unintentionally.

* * *

Pluto in the 10th house Opposition Mars; Mars is a co-ruler of the 3rd house: To accomplish his mission, most likely, any self-seeking aims were thoroughly calculated. The best for everyone is possibly desired by him. If heads of groups, or others, demand more than Nixon is willing to give, setbacks and problems can occur. If people are coercive or dictative toward him, they are likely to be in trouble. His reaction to this treatment tends to be one of anger, resentment and complete rebellion.

Pluto in the 10th house Opposition Mars in Sagittarius and Mercury in Capricorn in the 4th house: Dissensions, strife and quarrels can occur in his home when he has a meeting, or is involved with antagonistic people. He tends to speak up by making snap judgments, blurting his words out, being blunt and aiming his arrow on whoever is in the pathway. His statements might be too impulsively made.

Nixon can be rude, use bad language and fly off the handle. These courses of action would be due to his impatience with people who are slow, or ignorant—it's when intellect isn't used. He may feel that they are wasting his valuable time with trivial and nonsensical matters.

When his temper is shown by these preceding traits, he is likely to attract difficulties. His temperamental outbursts shortly subside—and that's when he has a personality change like a Jekyll and Hyde—from hot to cold.

To discover a way out, and avoid tensions with others, he has to scrutinize what he blew up about. His new approach will be words which are likely to be restricted and evasive. Wit, tact and diplomacy will probably be utilized. With his reserved air, he may appear to people that he's covering up his errors.

These temper tantrums can be made known and create damage to his name and career; especially, if wiretapping, tapes, transcripts, or illegal activities are involved. In these areas, the press will have a field day—so will the other news media.

Pluto in Gemini in the 10th house Opposition Mars in Sagittarius and Mercury in Capricorn-both in the 4th house: Nixon may feel impatient with reporters, groups, leaders of industry or labor unions, those who have a cause or those on specific committees and commissions.

A quick conclusion will probably be his goal; if it doesn't occur, his hastiness can cause a problem with those he deals with. While mediating, he tends to be stubborn; although, if he's in a hurry and the final result serves his purpose, he can be adaptable.

Pluto in the 10th house Opposition Mars, Mercury and Jupiter in the 4th house: Most likely, he will not allow anyone to dominate or manipulate him. It's possible that he will be unavailable to that person, or those groups who try.

* * *

Nixon should avoid blackballing, boycotting, framing, bribing, or placing others on a bad list; however, people could do those things to him. Either way, scandal and career difficulties can result bringing with them drastic action and changes.

* * *

Troublemakers, instigators and pesty people who oppose his ambitions, aims and desires can possibly be taken care of in due course. It's possible that measures are taken with those who try to coerce him.

Before Nixon makes any changes, or takes action, he is likely to weigh all of the pros and cons involved; however, if he jumps into things too fast without first thinking things through, he can wind up in a terrific jam. His psychic ability should be utilized at this time.

There tends to be a powerful force to his personality which makes him probably feel compelled to follow his convictions. It's possible that he can tune in to all of those people who are against him.

Nixon tends to have the courage to compete and verbally attack any group or person who threatens him, or interferes in his business. He can probably face anyone. Perhaps, it's his nerve, guts and ability to thrive when challenged that spurs him onward.

Rivals, opponents and competition doesn't seem to bother him. Strategy is possibly planned so he will outdo everyone. Most likely, he is optimistic that he will win. He will probably fight all the way to maintain his position because he doesn't want any person, or cause, to defeat him.

* * *

Those who try to frame him, or to do something against him, should perhaps run for cover. He doesn't seem to scare easily. Anyone who desires to expose, blackmail, extort, threaten or intimidate him is probably headed for big trouble.

It's possible that he will break and violate rules to gain his desired end. He may believe that it's in the best interest of all concerned.

He could play both ends against the middle to discover what he needs to know to come out on top. It's possible that he keeps statistical records on people. If necessary, he may use the information. He tends to go to lengthy means to stay in the position he feels he has earned—the Presidency.

CHAPTER FOUR

Money

Three planets in the Wealth houses: Nixon's major concerns can be business and wealth.

Venus, the ruler of the 2nd house of money, is located in the 6th house of labor: The performance of a job well done is more important to him than the money earned.

Venus rules the 2nd house, is located in the 6th house and is Square Saturn: Nixon could possibly take a decrease in pay, if there are shortages and money problems in a business or with the nation.

Venus rules the 2nd house and is located in the 6th house and is Sextile Jupiter which is in the 4th house and co-rules the 7th house: He tends to attract great wealth. Money may come easily to him. His earning capacity can be enormous. Nixon can amass vast personal holdings.

There are times when he doesn't care about money. He tends to believe that he will be alright. And he will. This aspect indicates a last minute saving grace.

* * *

Good fortune can be gained through social contract. People probably like his cheerful, confident and optimistic outlook. Because of it, they can be favorably disposed to deal with him in business.

* * *

He tends to spend currency foolishly to please and help others, or to have fun by living it up in plush restaurants and expensive living quarters. His motto may be to go first class all the way. Nixon can be a big tipper.

* * *

Real estate deals or partnerships can bring wealth. His money could possibly increase through selling, financing, banking, merchandising, law suits or art objects.

31

Venus rules the 2nd house and is Square Saturn in the 9th house: A tendency to accumulate, or lose, money. At times, he will probably worry needlessly about money.

If Nixon is too cautious toward financial investments, or delays real estate or foreign currency transactions, a personal loss of money can possibly occur.

On occasion, he could have a lack of confidence when trading and negotiating with overseas enterprises. This negativity could be due to a country's currency devaluation.

* * *

If Nixon placed his money in a foreign bank, or Swiss account, it's possible that he would tend to worry about it's discovery.

* * *

His taste in clothes may not vary much. Nixon's chief concern is probably to make a neat, reserved and nice appearance. Practicality is probably used in the selection of his suits. Good quality, stylish and expensive clothes may satisfy his desires. The latest fad may not appeal to him although it may interest him.

* * *

Cuff links and other expensive jewelry could be accumulated through the years. He probably takes extra good care of all of his personal belongings.

* * *

On long distance trips, or in foreign lands, it's possible that he's tight with spending cash. To travel with actual money could make him quite apprehensive and too fearful that it might be lost or stolen.

* * *

Business or campaign advertising could cost him plenty of sleepless nights. It could bother and worry him, if he has a loss in these areas. To avoid this problem, he may carefully plan and scrutinize in advance every dime to be spent on these projects.

Venus rules the 2nd house and is Sextile Jupiter, which co-rules the 7th house and is located in the 4th house; Venus is Sextile Mars; Mars rules the 8th house and is Semi-sextile Uranus in the 5th house: If he shares in com-

32

munal stock, or any joint business venture, opportunities for his finances to increase are most probable.

Venus rules the 2nd house, is in the 6th house and is Sextile Mars: Nixon can competitively go after money and drive deals through. By his using initiative and aggressive action, good chances for attracting financial backing, loans or business transactions can result.

* * *

Disbursements made on property he buys, or sells, can be dealt with while he's at home or away on a short distance trip. While on a short jaunt could be when he decides, one way or another, to take action with his finances.

Venus is in the 6th house and rules the 2nd house is in a Semi-square to the Sun in the 5th house, Sun in the 5th house and the Sun rules the 12th house: Nixon may make anonymous donations to charity. Contributions could be made at the suggestion of a wife, daughter, employee, politician, industrialist, or a person in an authoritative position. Secretly, it may annoy him to hand out money in this fashion. Most likely, to please others, he will give the money away without complaining.

Four planets and the ASC are in Earth signs; Venus rules the 6th house and is Sextile Jupiter and Mercury in Capricorn and is Square Saturn: His feet tend to be planted firmly on the ground when huge financial transactions are involved. Nixon is interested in making a profit; therefore, he employs conservative means and doesn't become foolishly carried away.

Sun in the 5th house rules the 12th house and is Semi-square Venus which rules the 2nd and 6th house: It's possible that he can become involved in secret financial ventures with people who are powerful, influential, wealthy, or who work under him in rank. These transactions may take place privately behind closed doors, or while entertaining and socializing.

Nixon may be easily disappointed with these personal deals. His pride and ego can be bruised if these people use him, or are unappreciative of his kindess and desire to help them. He tends to give in to the easy way out where money is concerned.

Perhaps, he will introduce people to each other so that they may help one another. In the end result, for being a good guy, he could be blamed for whatever occurs. It's possible that he is NOT *guilty* of ALL of the accusations thrown at him but, he could feel hurt and annoyed. This sensitive reaction is probably a closely guarded secret which is not discussed with anyone. Therefore, because of it, no one will ever be the wiser.

Whenever he gives a gift to someone who is close to him, he probably expects the person to respond gleefully. If this doesn't happen, his disappointment and touchiness would possibly be covered up.

If he is cheated in a restaurant, he will probably pay the bill graciously without a fuss. Perhaps, he doesn't like to bicker when out in the public.

Venus rules the 2nd and the 6th house and is Square Saturn in the 9th house and is Sextile Jupiter; Jupiter rules the 4th and co-rules the 7th house: Lawsuits may be costly whether they are taken to court, or are settled out of it. The enormous price paid for a lawyer will probably be worth it, because with the attorney Nixon could be saved from a personal appearance.

Real Estate

Mercury and Jupiter in Capricorn in the 4th house; Saturn in the 9th house and co-rules the 5th house and is Inconjunct Mercury: Foresight can be employed by Nixon with real estate purchases. He tends to hold on to land— it's his security. Owning property can give Nixon a steady, secure, contented and happy feeling.

Pluto in the 10th house Opposition Mars, Mercury and Jupiter in the 4th house; Pluto Trine Venus which rules the 2nd house; Venus Sextile Mars, Jupiter and Mercury in the 4th house: He could possibly be extremely ambitious to own more than one piece of property—an abundance of land. The more acreage that he possesses, the better he feels, and the more confident he can become.

His best areas for investment can be motels, hotels, shopping centers, office buildings, condominiums, and large parcels of land which can be subdivided.

Venus rules the 2nd house and is Sextile Jupiter which rules the 4th and co-rules the 7th house: It can be to Nixon's advantage to meet as many people as possible. His real estate holdings might possibly increase through social contact. Potential partnerships, or hints and tips on investments, could be in the air and discussed while he attends a party.

Enormous profits can be made when he sells real estate. *NOTE:* To do so, this aspect or another with Jupiter should be in by progression.

Pluto in the 10th house Opposition Jupiter in the 4th house; Jupiter co-rules the 7th house: Nixon is, most likely, skeptical of people. Before he leaps into any business transaction, he will probably seriously weigh all the pros and cons.

* * *

Real estate corporations can be to his advantage; however, they might pose a slight problem. Most likely, in deals of this nature, Nixon will desire to be the top man and own the major portion of the business. Otherwise, he could be afraid that those in control will dictate to him.

Saturn in the 9th house is Inconjunct Mercury in Capricorn and Mars in Sagittarius in the 4th house; Mercury is Opposition Pluto in the 10th house which co-rules his 3rd house: If he purchases property while in public office, he will, most likely, use care and caution. Fear of scandal, bad publicity and his career being ruined could hang over his head. However, nothing much may come of this desire to restrain himself from leaping into quick transactions. Any property deal will probably make the newspapers, and other news media; especially, if it involves his brothers.

* * *

Stock Market and Gambling

Sun in Capricorn in the 5th house Trine Saturn; Saturn is a co-ruler of the 5th house: Nixon, most likely, doesn't like to take any unnecessary risks with investments in the stock market. He probably prefers a sure thing. If he speculates, or places any money in this field, he will possibly analyze all of the facts and weigh the hazards regarding each company on the exchange.

Some favorable areas for investment are: Blue chips; mines; ores; natural resources; basic materials or lumber; lead; the foreign exchange.

Uranus in Aquarius in the 5th house: His stock will never probably be on a steady level—it can go up and down. When he buys securities, if he uses his intuition he could probably do quite well. If Nixon says, "I KNOW this stock is going to do well"—that's when he should invest.

Any company which is going to develop new products, plants, or become involved in research, can possibly benefit Nixon.

Uranus in the 5th house Semi-sextile Venus which rules the 2nd house: Children, or loved ones, can give him many unusual ideas for investment purposes. Also, valuable information can be received when he attends social gatherings.

Some favorable areas for investment are: Electronics, computers; inventions; electrical gadgets; appliances; automobiles or modern equipment.

Uranus in the 5th house Semi-sextile Jupiter in the 4th house: Tin, or products which contain it, might be advisable for Nixon to buy shares in.

Uranus in the 5th house Semi-sextile Mars which rules the 8th house: It might benefit Nixon to own securities in the following: Liquor; ammunition; machinery or firearms; knives; implements of construction or for destruction purposes; surgical instruments.

Sun in the 5th house Semi-sextile the Moon in the 6th house: Gold and silver can be profitable to buy in bullion cube or certificate form.

Sun in the 5th house and rules the 12th house in an Opposition to Neptune in the 11th house; Neptune co-rules the 7th house: Any type of stock which is supposed to bring overnight riches, make a killing and promise a fortune—Nixon, most likely, can discount 90% of what is promised.

Disappointments may take place on fantastic schemes, big deals and huge projects. The investment will probably not turn out as promised, or as Nixon imagines it is going to be. It's possible that the facts and companies are misrepresented, or fraud may occur.

Any investment which is too good to be true, he has to be leery of; otherwise, he could be completely fooled. Any deceptions may come through his friends, men, executives, leaders of industry, or people of affluence.

It's possible that Nixon will exaggerate, tell a fib, half-truth, or make false statements so he can promote others to purchase a particular stock.

The purpose for this type of action could be that if people bought the said security, the price may rise, and Nixon could sell his shares at a profit.

If this occurs, the others involved might be left holding the bag. As a result, Nixon could lose a few buddies. It's also possible that his pals didn't invest, but he did. If the stock fizzles, he could be quite disappointed.

Debts—Taxes

Mars in Sagittarius is the ruler of the 8th house: He's most likely a person who likes to pay his debts, taxes, loans, insurance or trust fund payments "right now," as quickly as possible.

Mars is the co-ruler of the 3rd house and rules the 8th house and is in an Opposition to Pluto in the 10th house: His temper can be easily aroused if an investigation is made on his investments or taxes. Groups who attack him could bring attention and bad publicity to him and his brothers. Loans and property deals can also be sore areas when brought before the public.

Mars in the 4th house, rules the 8th house and is Opposition Pluto in the 10th house and in an Inconjunct to Saturn in the 9th house and is Parallel the MC (the MC rules the 10th house cusp): Nixon can evade paying some of his taxes; however, he could fear being caught. All penalties and fines will probably be quickly paid. Possibly, he feels that the less publicity, the better. Scandalous headlines in the newspapers, or in any other news media, could lead to a court action; therefore, he will probably try to avoid anything that could possibly attract a problem.

Mars in the 4th house, co-rules the 3rd and rules the 8th house and is in a Conjunction and Parallel with Jupiter which is in the 4th house: His biggest headache can be mortgages on property, payments on taxes, insurance, or loans. He tends to attract heavy debts and expenses. With them all, he could probably care less.

It's possible that he will hurriedly borrow large sums of money for the acquisition of property. Enormous payments (balloon) can be involved.

Mars rules the 8th and co-rules the 3rd house and is Sextile Venus; Venus rules the 2nd house: If anyone owed Nixon any money, he will possibly speak up and ask for it. Although, on occasions he may take the easy way out and be kind, considerate, and wait until the person has the necessary legal tender.

Other People's Money

Mars rules the 8th house and is Sextile Venus which rules the 2nd house: Perhaps, Nixon's easiest avenue to approach potential backers in business, or with a political campaign, is through social contact. When he is kind and charming, people will probably desire to help him.

* * *

It's possible that when Nixon spends the public's money on entertainment or any social affairs, it is not overdone.

Mars in the 4th house rules the 8th house and is in an Opposition to Pluto in the 10th house: If he uses forceful tactics on others to obtain a loan, or backing, problems will most likely result. However, Nixon will probably continue to persist with the individual until he wins.

* * *

Enormous sums of the taxpayer's money can be spent on nuclear power, atomic energy experiments or equipment, arms, ammunition, space projects or chemicals.

The public, political parties and gorups could possibly oppose and rebel against Nixon's ideas for heavy expenditure of the taxpayer's money in these areas. Perhaps, this will not stop Nixon because he tends to be compulsively invovled in these matters.

* * *

Nixon will probably verbally fight to obtain money for the underdog, handicapped, minorities, underprivileged, or for those who receive a pension, medicare, social security, unemployment insurance, subsidy, or grants.

* * *

The national debt, with the way Nixon spends, can probably pile up fast and heavily. Groups can possibly go against him, if he grants huge loans that they don't believe in. If they try to stop him from taking action, he could rebel. It's likely that Nixon doesn't want anyone to dictate to him.

* * *

He can attract people who may investigate any unreasonable, excessive and inessential outlays, costs or squanderings of the taxpayer's money. Perhaps, Nixon will battle with them to the end. Bad publicity may result and possibly a loss of his power or position.

* * *

Strife can be attracted whenever Nixon becomes involved with labor unions or raising taxes. With these matters, he tends to be impatient and may desire to expedite everything as quickly as possible. If necessary, he might use force to have his own way, so he can push the necessary changes through. Any impulsive and demanding action, on his part, will probably create difficulty with people and can bring unfavorable publicity.

* * *

It's possible that the Nixon administration can use government agencies for political purposes, and spend the public's money for the same motives. The decision to do so is first weighed with all of the pros and cons analyzed, and once decided upon fast action can take place. Any underhanded schemes in these areas can bring him great difficulty.

* * *

Nixon can possibly be forced by others to become involved in shady deals or crooked transactions. Pressure could be applied by threats of exposure of one of his other past deals.

Conferences, about the preceding and the following, may be held in his home. If hush-hush money is brought up in a conversation, Nixon will probably briefly weigh the pros and cons about paying it out of his or other people's funds. Any pay-off deal will most likely be taken care of away from him or his house. It's not probable that he personally would be involved; he tends to leave this to others.

38

If anyone offered to pay Nixon hush-hush money for a favor, the reaction he has will probably be one of anger and deep resentment. He could possibly be so furious that he may feel compelled to expose the person to the world. However, before he takes any drastic measures, he will probably think it thoroughly through. He may think that the public would accuse him, misinterpret everything and dire repercussions could possibly result. As a result of this, Nixon will probably leave well enough alone.

Pluto in the 10th house in an Opposition to Mars, Mercury and Jupiter in the 4th house—Mars rules the 8th house: If Nixon is caught in an illegal activity, it will be brought to light because with Pluto in the 10th house, he could NEVER get by with a crooked deal.

All hell will probably break loose with an abundance of scandalous publicity. The end result is that Nixon will probably be the one blamed for the whole sordid affair. A loss of position might impend and a drastic change in his prestige could occur.

Sun rules the 12th house and is in an Opposition to Neptune in the 11th house; Neptune co-rules the 7th house: It's possible that Nixon does not know the whole truth about what is really transpiring in regard to pay-off deals. It could be that he prefers to be told only what's necessary about the details. However, if he does know anything, it's probable that he will keep it a secret as he does not want to involve himself or any friends in these affairs.

Mars rules the 8th and co-rules the 3rd house and is in an Opposition to Pluto in the 10th house; Mars is in an Inconjunct to Saturn in the 9th house; Mars is Sextile Venus in the 6th house: Aid to foreign countries will probably be cooly considered before Nixon takes any action with the taxpayer's money. Most likely, he will decide upon what is in the best interest for all concerned.

It's possible that Nixon has a strong and compulsive desire to help the needy, poor, underprivileged, or disaster stricken. He probably believes that by helping these people, universal brotherhood will be advanced a step further.

* * *

Mars rules the 8th house and is Sextile Venus in the 6th house and is in an Inconjunct to Saturn in the 9th house: Nixon's belief may be that the public's money, which is disbursed on entertainment for those in foreign countries, will establish good relationships and bring contacts which can bring favors and advantages at a later date.

CHAPTER FIVE

Foreign Deals
and Relationships

Pluto in the 10th house Semi-sextile and Parallel Saturn in the 9th house: Foreign nations can be of vast concern to Nixon. He will probably give them top priority. To do universal good, gain peace for all, and to work for the cooperation of all countries in world trade—these are possibly his ultimate goals.

Saturn in the 9th house, also co-rules the 6th house: He will, perhaps, advance slowly to achieve his aims. Nixon can lie in wait by remaining in the background and taking a back seat to members of his staff who represent him in other lands.

Delays, postponements and setbacks can occur. If they do, there are times when he may feel that all his efforts are in vain. It may appear to him that he's not making headway, advancing or stepping forward. He tends to believe that the worst is likely to happen.

Saturn in the 9th house Sextile Neptune in the 11th house; Neptune co-rules the 7th house: For peace and trade negotiations, if necessary, Nixon will probably retreat long enough to wait for the right approach and moment. It's possible that he considers timing to be an important factor in all transactions, especially those which can culminate his idealistic dreams.

Saturn in the 9th house Trine the Sun in the 5th house, rules the 12th house; Saturn Sextile Neptune; Neptune is in the 11th house and co-rules the 7th house; Saturn Trine the Virgo rising ASC: He tends to be practical stable shrewd, conservative and clever. Nixon can calculate to resist attack. These traits are probably used when he is trading or negotiating.

Perhaps, he is similar to a master chess player, and is cautiously watching the moves made by his opponent. All of the pros and cons are probably weighed and analyzed for every possible type of action and reaction. He tends to have the ability to arrive at the base of all problems.

Saturn in the 9th house, co-rules the 5th and 6th house and is Inconjunct Mercury; Mercury rules his 1st, 4th and 10th house: Bartering and dealing with international traffic, law, court, trade or any type problem can tend to be extremely serious matters to Nixon.

Once plans are made or foreign policies are signed and agreed upon, he will probably stick with them. It's possible that he will worry that others will not do the same.

Saturn in the 9th house, co-rules the 5th and 6th house: Saturn is Trine the Virgo rising ASC; Venus rules the 2nd house and co-rules the 9th house and is in the 6th house and Venus is Trine Pluto in the 10th house and Venus is Sextile Jupiter; Jupiter co-rules the 7th house: While in a foreign land, Nixon may appear serious, grim, humble, silent, self-collected, alert and on-guard with all that transpires. He tends to be friendly, warm, charming and carefree. These traits, combined with being cooperative for universal brotherhood and trade, can bring him good fortune. If he uses an optimistic attitude about these matters, and with enemies, luck will probably prevail.

Saturn in the 9th house, co-rules the 5th and 6th house and is Square Venus in the 6th house: There are times when Nixon probably doesn't feel in the mood to attend a social gathering. However, if duty calls he may attend, possibly be bored and feel dull. When this mood strikes, he will probably make an effort to appear contented, but to others he might look too reserved., staunch and somber. He can attract skepticism and distrust from those who he contacts; therefore, this cool appearance can possibly hinder his relationship with those in foreign countries.

Saturn in the 9th house Trine Sun in the 5th house: Business transactions and agreements made with heads of state can possibly make him proud of his ability to handle international affairs.

Saturn in the 9th house, co-rules the 6th house and is Semi-sextile and Parallel Pluto in the 10th house; Saturn is Trine Uranus in the 5th house; Uranus co-rules the 6th house; Saturn Trine Sun in the 5th house: Nixon can be seriously concerned about conservation of energy and the basic materials of life needed by the people of every nation. Modern projects, plans, labs and research in these areas might possibly be part of Nixon's world plans.

* * *

Possibly, one of his motives for a visit to foreign nations could be to discuss and make plans for the utilization of nuclear energy. Another reason may be to talk about missiles and outer space programs.

It's likely that Nixon can persuade heads of state to become interested in his up-to-date theories and to unite with the U.S. on joint ventures along these lines. These areas, as well as commerce, importing and exporting, are probably matters that Nixon wants universal cooperation with, so there will be improvements for all people and nations.

Saturn in the 9th house Square and Parallel the Moon in the 6th house: It's possible that Nixon can attract problems with the working class in other lands. They might not agree with his policies, rules, regulations, restrictions, limitations, cutbacks on the prices, or the heavy duty and taxes which are likely to be applied to the items they export to the United States.

As a result of Nixon's actions, along these lines, he can attract problems from all sides. The foreigners will probably have financial losses because his restrictions can endanger their livelihood. Nixon may feel that he must protect the American people from the invasion of foreign products so they can earn wages. With his stubborness toward these issues, he will most likely resist anyone who wants him to change the rules.

Saturn in the 9th house Square Venus in the 6th house; Venus rules the 2nd house and co-rules the 9th house and is Semi-square the Sun in the 5th house; the Sun rules the 12th house: The devaluation of the dollar can possibly be one of Nixon's biggest headaches. It's probable that he may take on added work and responsibilities so he can determine the best way to solve this dilemma. He may feel that it's his duty to tell the public to economize and patiently wait for the dollar to rise.

* * *

Once his various phases are employed, he probably believes that the economy of the country will be elevated. Secretly, he tends to worry about a depression.

Saturn in the 9th house Sextile Neptune in the 11th house; Neptune co-rules the 7th house; Saturn Trine the Sun in the 5th house, the Sun rules the 12th house; Saturn Square Venus in the 6th house; Saturn Trine the Virgo rising ASC: People in foriegn countries, possibly to Nixon, are not his personal enemies. He can be charming, friendly, polite, serious and a gracious host to them. Whenever he entertains or talks to them, he will probably use tact and diplomacy. He doesn't have to worry about whether he should trust them or not, because he most likely feels that many of them are against the U.S., and not him personally.

Saturn in the 9th house, co-rules the 6th house and is Semi-sextile and Parallel Pluto in the 10th house; Pluto co-rules the 3rd house; Saturn Trine the Virgo rising ASC: All trips can be cleverly organized by him and his aides. Because of the tight security, many restrictions can be placed on his travels. Every type of protection will probably be taken. All contingencies which can arise and every possibility of danger is carefully scrutizined. Nothing is likely to be overlooked.

The secret service and police, here and overseas, are carefully picked. When Nixon travels in foreign lands, he probably is constantly on guard, his eyes darting everywhere.

43

CHAPTER SIX

Scandals and Publicity

The majority of his planets are below the center line of the chart: It probably bothers Nixon that he doesn't always receive the proper credit for his meritorious actions. Others can take the spotlight away from him.

Pluto in the 10th house, co-rules the 3rd house: The areas in which Nixon will probably be remembered most in history, and which his fame and recognition tends to be in are: Wiretapping, tape recorders, transcripts, illegal activities, pay-offs, underhanded methods, sneaky tricks; dictating compulsory codes for others to follow; group involvement, civil liberties and rights, peace conferences and the ability to gain the cooperation of various nations or organizations to unite together for a common beneficial cause—brotherhood, nuclear power, and using atomic energy for conservation purposes, outer space programs, missiles.

Pluto in the 10th house, co-rules the 3rd house and is in an Opposition to Mercury in the 4th house; Mercury rules his 1st house: There possibly are times when Nixon desires to speak his thoughts while attending a meeting or when he's on T.V., the radio, or talking to the press. He may restrain from doing so because of his position and the possibility of maintaining a particular image. With this in mind, statements to the press may later be changed. Perhaps, Nixon feels it is the best for all concerned.

He will most likely rebel whenever people, the masses, political parties, groups or the press push him against the wall and try to force him into explaining the wiretapping, or any other matter.

Nixon probably has the courage to expose any crooked or shady transaction; however, the pros and cons will possibly be weighed. Decisions along these lines may be difficult for him to make. He most likely prefers to clarify matters; however, caution will probably rule the day.

Perhaps, if Nixon does speak up he will not tell everything. His part in a possible affair, or involvement with people of dubious means and character can ruin him. Nixon probably knows that a scandal could hurt everyone, including his relationships with people all over the globe.

Most likely, on the other hand, if he doesn't tell what he knows, the public and the press will probably say what they surmise to be true, and it's possible that some of their statements are wrong, or, perhaps, they are the actual facts.

Either way, being secretive or talkative, Nixon could have his reputation damaged. In his decision, he will probably have to choose the lesser of the two evils.

* * *

Nixon can receive publicity anytime he signs an important paper, document, deed or note, or makes an agreement with groups, or attends an important meeting.

Pluto in the 10th house, co-rules the 3rd house and is in an Opposition to Mercury and Mars in the 4th house: Whenever Nixon does an illegal deed it will probably be discovered. Disgrace and scandal can follow. If the Mafia, a large business organization, or an industrial concern is involved in the crooked operation, the stage and spotlight possibly will be Nixon's, day and night, until the affair is cleaned up or he resigns.

* * *

Talk, gossip and a downfall of prestige can occur if he takes part in hush-hush affairs, such as: Political racketeering, extortion and shakedown of the medicine, drug or food industry. If Nixon becomes involved in corruption with syndicates, or infringements of any nature, a partial collapse of his world may result. In a case like this, Nixon will probably take extreme measures and make some drastic changes.

* * *

If anyone tries to hold anything over his head, it probably won't last for long. He tends to rebel, especially if harassed. Pressure on him may possibly imply that he most likely will crack the case wide open.

Once he's riled, it might be his pleasure to expose everyone from the man at the top to the one at the bottom. It could be as of some inner force is directing him to take drastic action.

* * *

There is a possibility that he can collaborate involving tape recordings, wiretapping, or with a portion of a tape being erased, edited, altered or burnt.

If Nixon takes part in an activity of this type, it will become known and can bring the following results: Bad publicity, poison pen (hate) letters, the esteem in which he's held can be weakened, his power to mold conditions may be lessened, and a loss of job and a home could occur.

46

Pluto in the 10th house, co-rules the 3rd house and is in an Opposition to Mars in the 4th house; Mars rules the 8th house: He can attract problems from groups of people who oppose him, such as: Those involved in group movements, causes or bureaus, commissions, committees or labor unions.

If anyone in any of these realms attempt to threaten him by bugging devices, investigations or any other sneaky and underhanded tactic, that party will probably have to be on guard for Nixon's explosive temperamental reaction.

* * *

If anyone tried to do him in, most likely his first step will be to have an investigation done on the individual in question. Possibly, he believes that there is a skeleton in everyone's closet.

Once he has the reports, he will probably oust the enemy and defend himself. The spotlight could be focused on him, but he tends to have the courage to face any consequence.

Pluto in the 10th house, co-rules the 3rd house, and is in an Opposition to Jupiter in the 4th house; Jupiter co-rules the 7th house: Nixon probably feels confident that he can take care of anything that interferes with his plans. Perhaps, he believes that, most of the time, nothing will come of the actions, or coercion attracted from others.

* * *

He tends to be too sure of himself when it involves wiretapping, transcripts, tape recorders, real estate and business deals.

Pluto in the 10th house, co-rules the 3rd house, and is in an Opposition to Mercury and Jupiter in the 4th house: With certain newsworthy items, the press is likely to have a field day with Nixon. He may laugh at his bad publicity and say that he doesn't care about what's in the newspapers. His appearance can be deceiving because he has a tendency to cover up any distresss by a smile.

World-wide coverage *AGAINST* his better interests and self can disturb him to the point of obsession. He may feel that he MUST find a way to counteract everything said. Given time, *HE WILL!*

PART TWO

Nixon's Present and Future

The following aspect started July 7, 1973. The worst peak will be reached October 22, 1974. The discord will begin to lift after the peak date and will be completely out of his chart February 7, 1976.

ASPECT: Mars progressed Semi-square Jupiter natal.

By progression this is a mildly discordant aspect. In the natal chart, there is a Conjunction and Parallel aspect between these two planets. The natal aspects are neutral; however, since the progressed aspect is discordant, this aspect will work inharmoniously.

HOUSES INVOLVED:

The Mars influence—The sign Scorpio is on the 3rd house cusp (Mars is one of the rulers of Scorpio). The natal Mars is in the 4th house. The progressed Mars is in the 5th house. The sign Aries is on the 8th house cusp (Mars rules Aries).

The Jupiter influence—The natal and progressed Jupiter are in the 4th house, and the sign Sagittarius is on the 4th house cusp (Jupiter rules Sagittarius). The sign Pisces is on the 7th house cup (Jupiter is one of the rulers of Pisces).

Marriage Partner and Daughters

Disagreements about his extravagent spending, debts, or any exhorbitant spending of the public's money can bring minor upsets with those close to him.

With them, Nixon may feel annoyed. Stress and tension can build up, some of which he will probably keep within. Words can be uttered quickly, without thinking. Most likely, when he realizes what he has said, he may try to make up for any wrong doing.

Nixon is inclined to be extremely generous to those he loves. He wants them to be happy. Perhaps his feelings are that they deserve the best of everything.

If he purchases gifts for his cherished ones, he may be over charged. This can anger him inside, but outwardly he may appear that he doesn't care.

Nixon can be so busy that he doesn't have enough time to indulge in fun with his family. It may seem to them that he is taking them for granted. Nixon most likely is confident that they love him and understand his preoccupations. At a later date, he may try to make it up to them by entertaining them in some fashion.

On occasion, he may make arrangements to get together with the members of his family, but something may interfere—the telephone rings, or correspondence is received that needs fast action. He might feel irritated when this occurs, but Nixon will, most likely, keep it to himself.

* * *

His sex drive is strong. An abundance of sex can be indulged in. However, he may now be in a hurry and take the "I don't have the time" attitude. Quarrels can result which provokes him temporarily, but soon his mood will probably be happy-go-lucky.

Sports

During this time, his interest in athletics may wane because of his various trips, preoccupations, and necessity to study deals which can involve business with others, here or abroad.

Nixon might briefly glance at sporting events on television, but he may not want to just sit still and be a spectator. He might prefer to read and indulge in pleasurable pursuits with those he loves. To release any tension, he may go fishing or play golf. He can possibly desire to live it up and have a ball, but could be peeved with himself because he might not give in completely to his wish-inspired impulses.

Communications

Newspapers, magazines, documents or papers can be hurriedly scanned. Nixon may not have time to completely analyze all of his reading material. Impatience can be felt. He may find it easier and quicker to discuss these matters with others. Nixon may feel that talking on the telephone is a waste of his valuable time, especially if people are repetitious or carry on long, drawn out conversations. There's a tendency for him to snap at others and to cut conversations short. His temper can be easily aroused through messages received by phone or courier, whether he's at home or traveling.

* * *

Correspondence has to have immediate attention; otherwise he may become so irritable that while he is dictating his annoyance is shown.

During this time period his mail will probably continue to increase. Perhaps, he receives mostly unpleasant letters now, but he may act as if he doesn't care.

* * *

While signing papers, formal agreements, notes or deeds, his signature most likely is written hurriedly and his face could be beaming with confidence. If the signing involves agreements made with foreign nations, it will mainly be in the area of communications, transportation, education, or something which involves spending the public's money. Nixon probably figures that he is doing the right thing, and if the public disagrees, it may bother him that they don't go along with his wishes. If his opponents attack him, he most likely will (under his breath) mutter a few cuss words.

Enemies

Verbal clashes can occur in his home with any foes who try to attack him about his extravagant spending of the taxpayer's money. Little explosions may also take place with those who want him impeached. But a few moments later, Nixon will probably laugh off any quarrel. Perhaps, he feels that he is above and beyond reproach.

* * *

Carelessness and being too lenient with the secret service must be guarded. An assassination attempt may take place. It can be while entertaining, or being entertained, or while driving through a city in a motorcade, or while shaking hands with strangers. Whether it is a bomb, explosive, gun, knife, or physical attack, Nixon has to be careful of being over confident and taking chances.

* * *

He most likely has high expectations that all wars will cease. The public's money can be extravagantly spent toward aiding those in war-torn countries. His adversaries will probably bring his temper to the surface whenever they shout to the public that Nixon's generosity with those countries is unnecessary. During this time, he has to use caution whenever he speaks impulsively in defense of his actions.

* * *

To impress those he deals with in foreign nations, he may arrange costly amusements and entertainments. His mood will possibly be to have a good time and combine business with pleasure. Impatience can be felt if a social affair is too long and drawn out.

If Nixon doesn't throw a party for these people, he may compensate by being extravagant, impractical and carefree with the spending of the public's money. He might feel that he's Santa Claus and wind up paying an exhorbitant price for lavish gifts—like helicopters and cars. This may be Nixon's way of saying "thank you" to the people who have wined and dined him and agreed to his propositions. However, if the presents are given before any proposals have been agreed upon, Nixon may have high hopes that the gifts will ease tensions and have some bearing upon the other party going along with his aims.

His opponents will most likely attack him for this excessive spending. The press will have a field day writing about it, and Nixon could probably care less. If others call him on the carpet, his temper can be easily aroused.

* * *

Agreements on arms or any destructive weapons will most likely not be reached while this aspect is in his chart. Nixon will probably be over-confident that some type of a term will be consummated, but nothing much will come of his wishes.

NOTE: THIS SECTION APPLIES IF HE'S STILL IN OFFICE.

The Public's Money

Quick action can be taken with the taxpayer's money. Excessive sums may be loaned for foreign aid. These spending sprees of his can increase more as October 1974 is approached. Money may be spent toward large real estate investments, housing projects or anything dealing with land (the earth). There can possibly be some deal involving insurance companies and large structures being erected through them.

Other forms of disbursements might be on Medicare, unemployment insurance, pensions or social security. Nixon may see to it that an increase is allotted in these areas. As a result, he may have taxes raised.

* * *

Nixon's trips may cost the public enormous sums. His travels and expenditures can continue to increase.

He may grant subsidies to others. Nixon must guard against being independent, careless and over confident with how he handles the taxpayer's money. However, his desires might be for the betterment of others and relationships with those in foreign nations. Perhaps he expects, in the long run, that the returns will be much greater than the disbursements.

Through a lack of discrimination and being off in his calculations, the country may be in the red. The national debt can increase to higher amounts. Nixon probably feels like jumping into things "right now" and taking action before it's too late. Perhaps, he believes that he is doing the correct thing.

This is an unfavorable time for him to make hasty decisions and snap judgements which involve spending the public's money; but, if anyone mentions this to him, most likely, he will be contrary and not pay any attention to the antagonistic remarks made.

The Public

With a pleasant smile, Nixon now can enjoy face to face contact with the public. His over confidence with being so close to people will probably continue for a while.

With prices increasing, inflation growing stronger, Nixon tends to be optimistic that the high cost of living is nothing anyone has to be concerned about. Perhaps his feelings are that everything is going to be fine and that prices will drop. At this time, his thinking along these lines is in error.

Nixon will probably fight for his beliefs and maintain that the public will soon see a change. His exaggerated statements can turn people against him. He may be annoyed that others don't understand his motives.

The public most likely will be turned against him more and more if he continues granting huge loans. He should not be so magnanimous with placing this country in a bigger deficit than it already has. During this time, action of this type is not wise.

* * *

Public opinion polls are not likely to interest him at this time. If people provoke him enough, his irritation will probably show. Statements, with no punches barred, can be made. He has nerve and courage and is not afraid to telling the public or his antagonizers what he thinks; however, he may try to hold everything within.

During this time, he should use caution when speaking to others because any impulsive outbreaks of temper can create more difficulties. Perhaps outwardly, he feels that lawsuits and impeachment are not going to touch him. Inwardly, he is probably annoyed that they may.

* * *

Contracts and vows made by Nixon, or by others to him, may not be maintained. He can be angry if they aren't performed. The public may feel that he doesn't know what he is doing and that he is too trusting of the enemy.

Brothers

Nixon can be out of sorts with his brothers whenever they are in heavy debt, need a loan from him, borrow from a banking institution by using his name, or if they use him for any special favors.

Quarrels can ensue when they make foolish mistakes, especially if he co-signed a note or loaned them money to become solvent. Most likely, this is what will arouse his temper more readily than anything else.

This is not a favorable period for Nixon to become involved in any financial deals with his brothers, or to loan them any money. He can be extremely generous to them, at this time. His best bet is to lie low, be patient, and to remain silent. However, he may not follow this advice.

Nixon may become so excited over a large business project of theirs that he decides to invest his money in it. His optimism can increase as the development enlarges to greater proportions. The amount now gained will not be what he had anticipated—it will be less. In fact, there is no guarantee, at this time, of an increase coming through any investments with his brothers, especially if it involves real estate or the stock market.

Nixon's reaction to any losses will most likely be one of irritation, a "Well, we can't win them all" attitude. He will probably forget a loss and gladly look ahead to the next deal.

* * *

Nixon's brothers can cost him plenty financially. His enemies may use them as scapegoats. When his opponents attack his brothers publicly, Nixon may feel provoked. If they accuse his brothers, and him, of illegal activities, this annoyance can be greater than anything else.

Debts

Nixon may now desire more real estate or stock market holdings. His spirit tends to be that of a gambler. He can leap from one obligation to another and splurge on speculative ventures.

To go heavily into debt doesn't seem to fase him. The end result of a large return for his money is what he may be contemplating.

During this time, Nixon has to be careful of being too reliant upon the words of others. He tends to be too hopeful, in a hurry and can become irritated if he has to stop and analyze any of his business investments. Excesses have to be guarded against.

* * *

He may become peeved if he has to devote any time toward thinking about such trivial matters as debts. His bills can be paid quickly with enormous sums going towards interest payments on notes. If he has to borrow more money, aggravations are probably felt, but he will tend to keep them to himself. To his family, he may appear confident that all will be fine.

Real Estate

Nixon can go heavily into debt with real estate, shopping malls or plazas, condominiums, office structures or lots. He may take on more than he can handle. He tends to be overconfident. He may feel that now is the time to take action, before real estate prices rise.

* * *

This is not an auspicious time for him to expand with any type of real estate operation. Common sense may not be used. His judgment can be off balance. He may feel assured he will make a killing; therefore, he can spend too much money on everything he touches.

* * *

Impulsive, in a hurry to speculate and make a quick profit—that's Nixon. If he sells property now, he will not receive what the property is really worth.

* * *

It is not a favorable time for him to sign papers on any huge project. He may speedily make a decision to place his signature on the dotted line—Nixon's mood can be one of great optimism.

* * *

If he needs a backer or partner, he probably will be confident that one will be found without any difficulty. Nixon can brag to the person what a fantastic sum of money can be made on a particular real estate venture.

During this time period, Nixon is likely to make statements beyond the truth and exaggerate. As a result, everyone can jump on the band wagon, expecting to make a fortune. Money can be gained, but not as much as Nixon expects.

The risks and chances he takes now can prove to be hazardous. Nixon may not take the time to think things through. He can be too busily engaged taking action in too many areas.

If he has a building torn down or a new one erected, setbacks and complications can cost him enormous sums of money. Perhaps his reaction will be one of rage, which later turns into an attitude of, "Well that's one of the risks a person has to take in business." And with that, off he can go, not glancing back at a loss, but looking forward to his next deal, which he may think will yield him all the money he desires.

Stock Market

He should guard against impulsive speculation with the stock market, during this time. The money he expects to make will not be there. His assumptions are greater than his realizations. He's most likely to sell at the wrong moment. If he holds out until later, he can make a larger profit.

* * *

His main losses can be if he invests in stocks that involves machinery, surgical equipment, guns or any form of ammunition or destructive device.

Whenever a broker tries to talk him out of selling a particular stock, Nixon, being headstrong, stubborn, and in an "I know it all" mood, may not listen. If a loss occurs, he may be provoked, but will probably say to himself that he doesn't have the time now to think about these small matters.

If he has a ticker tape, he may take a quick glance at it now and then. His impatience and being pressed for time can make him not want to be bothered with it. Perhaps, if Nixon needs a quick decision with any stock, he will rely

56

more upon his broker than on the ticker tape. During this time, he has to guard against his own judgment and that of the broker.

* * *

Whenever he does margin buying, he may have to sweat it out to make the payment in time. It will probably be put off until the last minute. Perhaps Nixon will borrow the money from a lending institution, sell some of his stock, or mortgage his property.

Taxes

His taxes, he will most likely try to pay immediately, even if he has to borrow money to do so. Enormous sums can be paid out as the year ends. Taxes for him may increase—so can his deductions.

Home

Quick business trips can continue to keep him busy. Impatience may be felt in the home. He might feel doubtful about staying in any one place for long. During this time, he can move about from one residence to another.

* * *

The problems he attracts now are due to his own doing rather than that of outside forces. His rivals will continue to press for his impeachment. As they yell, Nixon's displeasure can be more noticeable. If he is impeached, he will not believe that it is really happening.

Health

His physical energy can be depleted because he overworks beyond need or necessity. He may feel drained, but will probably push onward. Nixon doesn't seem to care about his health as much as business.

* * *

All types of accidents can occur now. It's possible that he will walk too fast, not look where he's going, and bump into furniture, or will knock down objects. He must take care of tripping and falling. His ankles are weak.

He should guard against overdoing any muscular activity. If he overexercises, he might strain a ligament. His muscles tend to be flabby. Nixon may feel like tightening them up.

Nixon can gain weight from dinners, snacks, buffets, and any form of overeating. Stimulants, like coffee and liquor, do not agree with his system during this time period. Protein may be difficult to handle, especially meat and eggs. Fats can be a source of difficulty. He has to take care of excessive eating of butter, cream sauces, pastry, carbohydrates, spices, condiments, and hot (spicy) food—like hot sauces on Mexican food. Once this aspect is out of his chart, he can return to eating the preceding foods without attracting a problem.

His cholesterol count can be high. Blood clots, cysts, tumors, sores, rashes and hardening of the arteries can be attracted now.

It is not a favorable time for an operation. He may want to have one so he can get it over and done with; but his impulsive action can attract problems.

* * *

The following aspect started July 17, 1971. The best peak will be reached October 29, 1974. The harmony involved will start to lift after the peak has been reached, and will not leave his chart until December 17, 1977.

ASPECT: *Venus progressed Parallel Pluto progressed*

By progression this is a harmonious aspect. In his natal chart there is a Trine aspect between these two planets; therefore, this aspect is totally one of harmony.

HOUSES INVOLVED: *The Venus influence*... The sign Libra is on the 2nd house cusp (Venus rules Libra). The natal Venus is in the 6th house. The progressed Venus is in the 8th house. The sign Taurus is on the 9th house cusp (Venus rules Taurus).

The Pluto influence... The sign Scorpio is on the 3rd house cusp (Pluto is one of the rulers of Scorpio). The natal and progressed Pluto are in the 10th house.

Marriage Partner

He may try to be tender, warm, loving and kind to his wife. If he displeases Pat, he will probably go out of his way to make it up to her. There is likely to be a strong and intense tie between them, like a bond of mutual understanding.

Together, they can work as a wonderful team doing good for those close to them and to mankind. Patricia will most likely cooperate with him by going along with his commands and wishes. Nixon has wonderful luck which perhaps will partially come through his mate.

Socializing

During this time period, his charm at receptions, banquets and all social functions can bring him good fortune. He is well groomed, refined, courteous, amusing, cheerful and wishes others happiness.

58

Because he takes an interest in the affairs of others, information can be gained at these gatherings. Nixon has an innate ability to draw from people that which he needs to know. By tuning into others, he can surmise those who will probably favor his causes.

When he is pleasant and kind, Lady Luck will be at his side. She may appear as a business proposal, which, if accepted, may turn out as a profitable venture.

* * *

People connected with the United Nations can be fortunate for Nixon. Any deed which is beneficial for the universe may be discussed at receptions. If Nixon is pleasant and friendly now, others will respond by being cooperative and wanting to join in with his humanitarian efforts.

* * *

While in a foreign country, Nixon will probably beam as he is surrounded by congenial people. Crowds will tend to be friendly. Translators may be needed, but there can be a good rapport between Nixon and his hosts.

* * *

With food and drinks at parties, Nixon may take the easy way out and accept them, rather than hurting someone's feelings by declining. At these affairs, he can mix and mingle, for business purposes and fun.

* * *

Graciously, he may bestow compliments on anyone who has performed meritorious deeds, such as astronauts, cosmonauts, scientists. Also, he can be extremely nice to spies, policemen, the FBI, and the secret service.

Money

During this time, he can spend money on art, jewelry, clothes, and luxury items, such as heliocopters or any mode of transportation. Nixon tends to go first class and buys the best. These costly expenditures may be for himself, loved ones, or for people in foreign lands.

* * *

Nixon has been, and will probably continue to be (if he's still president), the recipient of some beautiful gifts from those abroad. He realizes that he cannot keep these treasures, but he may feel elated that the donators were so kind, considerate and thoughtful in giving them.

* * *

There is probably no end to his desire to amass material possessions. He may donate gifts, money, or his old clothes. His desire is to please others, which can include minorities, employees, and the underprivileged.

Usually his generosity knows no bounds when he tips a maid, valet, waiter, attendant, or any public servant. The good service received and the desire to help may be what motivates him to treat them in this fashion. He probably feels that they appreciate, and need, the money.

* * *

He is undoubtedly quite lucky now, and no matter how many money problems come, he can be saved at the last moment. If he has tenants, legal tender may arise from that direction. Mutual funds can pay him satisfactory dividends, when he needs the money. A group investment can pay off. Those who owe him cash may come through during this time. Backers will probably be behind him, if he needs them.

Banking institutions may favor him. Loans can be easy for him to obtain. If he feels impressed to ask for anyone's help along these lines, deals can wind up in his favor.

Taxes
He may take the easy way out and pay his taxes without any hassle. By being cooperate and paying fines and penalties, luck will probably result.

Its possible that a group of people may try to take him to court after he has settled his account with the Internal Revenue Service. While this aspect is in Nixon's chart, he most likely will continue to be saved by those who are on his side.

The Public's Money
Nixon can spend the taxpayer's money on research in medicine, nutrition, chemistry experiments, nuclear energy projects, and any area where better conditions for others may result. Grants can be received from tax exempt foundations for these humanitarian causes.

Funds may be raised for political parties, minorities, the underprivileged, the handicapped, or for any beneficial campaign. Banquets can be held for such purposes, and his attendance at them may help bring aid to others.

Foreign Countries

Now, it is to Nixon's advantage to travel abroad and to make wise affiliations with those who also want peace and brotherhood.

NOTE: This holds true if there are no discordant Moon progressed aspects, during the same time period.

* * *

Many long distance trips overseas, during this period, can prove fortunate. His traveling may continue, and favorable results can be noticeable. These jaunts might be to join forces with others for worldwide prosperity. They can be profitable when everyone cooperates for a mutual gain.

Mass production of products, with importing and exporting to and from all countries, may be part of the transaction. Negotiations can be made for uniform trade and/or currency. Buildings and structures which house and employ millions may be talked about. Nuclear energy can be discussed, and agreements signed accordingly. All types of future broadcasting (television, communication satellites and other advanced forms of news and educational media) may be talked over at these meetings.

* * *

The heads of state whom he visits will, most likely, give him credit for all of his past accomplishments. He now has them in the palm of his hand. Gossip, scandal and bad publicity does not interfere with their relationship.

Friendship and kindness can be exchanged on these trips or if others visit him. Nixon may have a good time socializing, taking the walking tours, watching the groups march, or relaxing.

His Aims

He may desire to aid others to accomplish a shared and useful objective which can be profitable to all countries. Nixon might feel the urge to achieve good for humanity, helping people, the community or a country. This may be accomplished through alleviating and lessening misery and pain in others.

Nixon can possibly better conditions through social security; pensions, unemployment insurance; medicare; socialized medicine; medicine; chemistry; atomic energy tests, nuclear energy and fuel (power plants as a chain all over the world); research; missiles; outer space programs to use energy in the cosmos; prefabrication or tract homes; health (food and diet) projects.

The people's money may be involved in these deeds. Loans can possibly be granted to foreign nations, so, they are able to perform their part in any one of these mass undertakings.

Nixon may plan business on a national and international basis. He can encourage industrial corporations to obtain branches in other countries. Perhaps on the agenda are mergers, franchises and patents which involve an exchange between people from all lands. Gradually, each country can have (under this plan) operations all over, which makes for friendly relationships and money in the bank for everyone. This mutual trust and cooperation between everyone cuts down on future wars and can be part of Nixon's idea for brotherhood and peace.

* * *

Civil rights, minorities and the underprivileged can bring luck to Nixon *now*, if he aids their causes. Through consultations and meetings with the various parties involved, good can come to everyone concerned. If a charity group becomes involved, or a foundation decides to grant money to assist those in need, Nixon will probably come out smelling like roses, especially if he appears on nationwide television and asks in a kindly manner for the public to help by supporting these causes.

* * *

If Nixon becomes involved, during this time, with labor union strikes, he may have luck when enforcing compulsory codes on others. The masses will most likely be in agreement with him (if there are no discordant Moon progressions to contradict).

Through charm and an interest in everyone, Nixon may try to persuade the labor union officials that he is doing the just thing by protecting the majority of people from a costly strike. His intervention can possibly be a benefit to all concerned.

Performance of His Job

Nixon likes to be well organized. He may use the latest devices and inventions to aid his subordinates in their work. Some peace and harmony can be felt with many of those who labor under him.

Good service may be received from his employees when he is kind, generous, cooperative and works with them as part of a team. They can possibly furnish him will all type of information, statistical reports and data on any investigation which was undertaken. This may later be used to his advantage. In appreciation for their efforts, Nixon may invite them to social functions, give them a gift or bonus.

* * *

If an intermediary continues to negotiate for Nixon, luck will possibly result. Having a go-between and giving him complete cooperation may be one of

Nixon's smart moves. For better results, Nixon should be pleasant and friendly to him. He should show his representative how appreciative he is for his efforts.

Socializing and traveling together can prove fortunate for both parties. These actions are likely to continue even stronger as the new year (1975 approaches. (NOTE: The preceding is if Nixon is still in public office; otherwise, he could travel with his entourage and attend many parties.)

Any lecturing or talking on television, radio or the public platform now can be lucky for him, if he does it in a congenial and pleasant manner. His opinions and beliefs may be favorably received. (The preceding is likely if there are no unfavorable progressed Moon aspects in to contradict the latter paragraph.)

Wiretapping and Court

The costly sums of money being paid to a lawyer (or group of lawyers) can be well worth it. If he cooperates with them and others who are on his side, good fortune with the tapes and court may result.

* * *

If he is impeached and appears in court from October 1974 to April 1975, the verdict will probably be in his favor. He may be saved at the last minute through a good legal team behind him and because he is cooperative. Many people can come to his aid during this time, especially those who work under him now or did in the past.

* * *

The following aspect started in June of 1972. There will be two peaks. The first peak is April 15, 1975. The second peak is Feb. 17, 1977. The discord will start to lift after the last peak has been reached. The aspect will leave his chart November 17, 1980.

ASPECT: *Venus progressed Parallel Saturn natal and progressed*

By progressions this is a neutral aspect. In the natal chart there is a Square between these two planets; therefore, the aspect is one of discord.

HOUSES INVOLVED: *The Venus influence* ... The sign Libra is on the 2nd house cusp (Venus rules Libra). The natal Venus is in the 6th house. The progressed Venus is in the 8th house. The sign Taurus is on the 9th house cusp (Venus rules Taurus).

The Saturn influence ... The sign Capricorn is on the 5th house cusp. (Saturn rules Capricorn.) The sign Aquarius is on the 6th house cusp (Saturn is one of the rulers of Aquarius). The natal and progressed Saturn are in the 9th house.

Loved Ones

During this time period his emotions may be keyed-up, but he can repress his innermost feelings. This may be toward pets, children, or anyone he loves.

* * *

The love feelings are there for Patricia, but Nixon has difficulty in expressing tender words. He may not be very demonstrative now, due to worries and concerns which involves the security of those he holds dear. His mind can be preoccupied with: possible impeachment hanging over his head; debts bugging him; delays with foreign nations on important agreements he had wanted signed; or, the depression in this country.

* * *

If he travels without his wife, he will most likely miss her. However, if he takes her with him on his trips, due to the time lag, fatigue can make him less romantic. Lovemaking, in this case, may drain him of necessary energy. He can withstand temptation with sex, or if anyone tries to lure him into a love affair.

A misunderstanding may occur with a loved one regarding debts, taxes, money, travel and gifts. He can be practical with those he cherishes, although at times he will go in the opposite direction.

Under this aspect, he cares very deeply for his wife, daughters, and son-in-laws. If he ever lost anyone close to him, a guilt feeling would take place. It's possible that he would blame himself for not paying more attention to them. His suffering would be in silence.

Socializing

During this time, he has moments when he may not want to be bothered by attending social functions. Whenever he is invited to a party which will *not* benefit him, he most likely will decline. Nixon doesn't like to hurt people's feelings by saying "No" to important parties, especially if it is in a foreign country. Diplomacy can be used at these affairs.

* * *

If he's in pain (due to health problems), or feels dull, he may feel that he still must make an appearance and smile; especially, if it's an important social gathering.

* * *

With some people, he may feel ill-at-ease. It can be that these individuals do not measure up to his expectations, or the reverse. With them he tends to be quiet and cautious. He may not say much, but will probably listen to their conversations.

Nixon probably doesn't trust everyone he meets. It is wise for him to be on guard now with those who try to use flattery because they may desire to use him.

Health

Lack of energy may be due to travel, overwork, negative thoughts and too much emotion held within. His anxieties can exhaust him regarding impeachment, debts and the handling of the taxpayer's money.

* * *

While on an overseas trip, he can be in pain, unless he is on pain-killer pills. No one will know that he's not feeling well because he doesn't like to bore others with illnesses, or waste his time and energy discussing them.

* * *

Inflammation of the veins (phlebitis) may continue to bother him as April 1975 and March of 1977 approaches. This comes partly as a result of eating the wrong foods, constipation and a lack of vitamins C and E, calcium and minerals (Potassium and zinc, etc).

His circulation can get worse if he is not careful of his diet. Sweets and carbohydrates should be eliminated during this time. Whenever he indulges in them, he should notice how different he feels afterwards.

* * *

Blockages in his colon can cause the constipation problem, and may be partly responsible for the inflammation of the veins. Too many acids can be in his system. He can be prone to catching cold, or having throat problems. Nixon may have losses of hair, or skin blemishes, at this time.

NOTE: An operation will not rid his system of the poisons he is unable to eliminate properly.

If he wants to see fast results on his health improving, colonic irrigations might be advisable.

Work

A great concern for the future can dwell constantly on his mind; he tends to secretly worry that he will be impeached and lose his job.

* * *

If he's still president, perhaps, the assistance he receives from a few of his staff members will leave much to be desired. With these people, he may not be so generous or friendly. His aides, he may feel, cannot all be trusted. Due to past hurts and bitter experiences, he has learned that he should constantly be on guard against any future developments along the same lines.

NOTE: Most of the time, while this aspect is in, his suspicions will probably be correct.

One by one, his staff can continue to resign (if he's still in power), or he can possibly lose them through other channels. Nixon, most likely, knows how to slowly ease a person out of office. One method may be to cut down on the individual's duties. This, he may feel, will weaken the aide's power. If Nixon attempts this action, he will possibly have his own burdens increase, unless he turns the chores over to another staff member. However, it's the end result that may matter to Nixon.　　* * *

Ponderous responsibilities may weigh him down now. Because of them he may appear disinterested and indifferent to the problems which arise in connection with his position. However, limitations as to what he has power to do may hold him back and bring affairs to a momentary standstill.

Most likely, Nixon will not allow this to stop him. Instead he will probably add on more tasks for himself. While traveling, he may use his valuable time to work. He possibly has moments when he wishes that he could be like other people and sit back, relax and enjoy the flight. But an inner force seems to be pushing him ahead.

Nixon is similar to a master chess player, plotting each move. He's now employing, possibly, his greatest strategy. Everything he attempts is premeditated if it involves those in foreign countries, taxes, the public's money, impeachment, his job or reputation. He probably feels that he must have these affairs result in his favor; therefore, many of his plans can be scheduled for later dates.

* * *

NOTE: The following applies if he's still President:

Perhaps, Nixon has patiently waited for the opportune moment to take a trip abroad, at the taxpayer's risk. His purpose may be to avoid future wars, maintain peace and exchange trade. Any loss in these directions, he will probably shun. Gains can be uppermost in his mind.

Some snags and bottlenecks can take precedence with each trip; however, Nixon probably feels that with each visit he is slowly coming closer to his goals. On occasion, he may think that he's not making headway. But he, most likely, will not allow this type of negative thinking to hold him back from continuous trials and errors.　　* * *

Compliments might make him feel that he is appreciated; therefore, the approval of others is probably important to him. A pat on the back can possibly make him work that much harder.

The Public

His influence to sway and have control over the populace can be lessened due to his tax problems, debts, financial involvements, foreign travels, job or labor performed, a possible court case, and luxury gifts given with the public's money.

Appearing cool, Nixon will probably remain silent on these issues. It's possible that he doesn't want to talk about them. Within, he may feel hurt, worried and disturbed by what others think of him. To serve his country and protect the American people, he may feel is his necessary duty, one he thrives on. He does care about the country, but on a public platform, or in the home, he is not a person who shows his emotions, feelings or thoughts.

There's a tendency for him to be cautious and reserved whenever he publicly states his beliefs and opinions. If he could change from the settled way of speaking and try to show mirth, understanding and warmth, he may not attract so many people against him.

* * *

Foreign Relationships

Obstacles and delays in negotiating can depress Nixon (if he's still the President). If an agreement is signed, he may worry that it may not be fulfilled. Not everyone he deals with is trusted, but with his natural diplomacy no one is likely to discover it.

* * *

NOTE: The following applies if he's still President:

If Nixon tries to block or ruin any transaction that his go-between has accomplished with another nation, hindrances can arise in their relationship. He may lose an intermediary, if he isn't careful. Nixon may suspect this; therefore, he probably handles the person with kid gloves. Any compliments he bestows could be done in a detached manner.

It's possible that Nixon envies his representative's diplomacy, tactics and ability to negotiate; or, it may be that he's suspicious of the person's ambitions. It can be difficult for him to show his feelings to the individual for fear of being hurt by another member of his staff. This whole attitude, on Nixon's part, can create a barrier between their becoming close.

* * *

Whenever necessary, Nixon can be practical. He probably does not entirely desire to give luxury gifts with the taxpayer's (or his) money at stake. However, for future relationship and gain, he may believe that it is the best way to handle a situation.

NOTE: The following applies if he's still President: Disagreements with many of his aides can create a delay with granting loans to other countries. Before everyone is in complete accord, further stallings or postponements can take place. It may seem, to Nixon, that: Some of his staff members have a lack of understanding for those in need; their business judgment is off because they don't, perhaps, realize that they are throwing good diplomatic relationships out the window.

* * *

Money

NOTE: The following applies if he's still the President:

Most likely, Nixon has financial worries, not only of his own, but with the U.S. deficit. He tends to be thrifty on small items, and spends foolishly on larger ones.

Prices may be rolled back, frozen, fixed at a set amount, with more restrictions for everyone. Perhaps this is the only measure that Nixon thinks will work. He may believe that there is a depression, but he most likely will not allow himself to say it outwardly. If he does, he may be afraid that the panic button will be pushed by the American people.

* * *

The devaluation of the dollar may be a crisis to Nixon. To overcome the problem, procedures can be planned and economic measures taken. However, everyone involved may wait for the right moment to take action. It can be a slow process.

NOTE: The preceding may continue until this aspect reaches its last peak date. The above applies whether he is, or is not President. The economy of the United States can still effect him, regardless of his position.

Restrictions placed on importing and exporting products can be lessened or tightened by Nixon. This can create a problem. For instance, if they continue to be heavy, it's possible that international trade will be stopped. This implies that those who tend to gain will have their money blocked.

If Nixon lowers the custom duties and taxes, the national income can be thrown for a loop. With the U.S. budget operating in the red, Nixon knows the United States needs more revenue. He probably wants both sides of the issue to be ahead; however, he may feel helpless in making a move, or changing his actions once a decision is made. His judgment can be off-balance now, while this aspect is in his chart.

NOTE: The preceding two paragraphs applies if he's still the President of the USA.

* * *

Whenever he has a spare moment to think, heavy debts, taxes and loans (the public's or his) can possibly be dwelled on for too long.

The money spent extravagantly on gifts, entertainment or travel can give him a few sleepless nights, wondering whether he really was in the right.

* * *

In his innermost thoughts, he probably believes that he doesn't receive a just reward for all of his hard labor and daily personal sacrifices. But he most likely realizes that money is not as important to him as his duty to serve. Therefore, he can remain silent whenever these negative ideas creep to the surface of his mind.

* * *

Nixon can go heavily into debt, whenever he delays any court case. He may feel that the money spent is not as vital as his remaining President of the United States.

* * *

This is a difficult time for him to *accumulate* legal tender in a bank account. In it comes, and out it goes. Risky ventures can place a strain on his budget. Avenues where he expected money may not, at this time, come through.

Payments to or from others can be late. If a tenant owes him, he may worry that foreclosure measures will have to be taken. If he has to take action in this direction, he knows that the court proceedings can take time, or be delayed. Because of this, Nixon most likely will patiently wait for the tenant to pay him.

* * *

Some of his securities may go down. If the stock continues in this direction, Nixon may decide to buy some more, at a lower price. However, he may feel that the market is risky and a gamble is too hazardous. With this in mind, he may be afraid to plunge too deeply. However, if greed sets in, he may take a chance.

* * *

Taxes

Tax evasion can cost him money in lawyer's fees, fines and penalties. He may be concerned that he will be taken to court and if he loses the case, will possibly have to pay more.

NOTE: If he appears in court for tax problems, while this aspect is in, more fines are likely to be charged.

* * *

Further tax deductions may be desired; however, Nixon can be afraid to take a big chance on any items which are questionable. With accountants, or lawyers, his past trust may be ended, or Nixon may decide that he should scrutinize everything more carefully in the future.

* * *

The following aspect starts July 20, 1974. It reaches a peak July 21, 1975 and will leave his chart July 21, 1976.

ASPECT: *MC progressed Inconjunct Sun natal*

By progression this is a neutral aspect. In his natal chart, the Sun and the MC (an angle) are in a parallel, which is also a neutral aspect; therefore, this aspect will work as inflated desires with deflated results. Nixon will feel pleasant one moment, and unpleasant the next. A rather "blah" mood.

HOUSES INVOLVED: *The MC influence.* . . The natal MC is the 10th house cusp. The progressed MC is in the 11th house until February 26, 1976, at which time it will enter the 12th house.

The Sun influence . . . The natal Sun is in the 5th house. The progressed Sun is in the 7th house. The sign Leo is on the 12th house cusp (The Sun rules Leo).

Career

Nixon may gradually start to think more about a new career for himself. Perhaps, there are moments he wants to go into his own business, but later he changes his mind.

Most likely he feels that he must be in a profession where self-respect, authority and power are involved. A distinguished position, like being an ambassador, can possibly intrigue him. It may sound dignified, but when he thinks of the entertainment involved, he will probably close the door on that area.

His pals may suggest various enterprises for him. At the moment some of these areas can interest him. Later, he possibly feels "blah" toward these ventures.

Future partnerships with friends may be thought about, or actually discussed. The ideas, most likely, will little by little disappear, unless Nixon takes immediate action with them and forms a quick association.

* * *

There may be moments when he feels let down because he hasn't received credit for his various accomplishments. Yet he may give awards to others who merit them. The latter can attract small amounts of publicity.

* * *

Meetings can take place behind closed doors with heads of state, politicians, or those of wealth and influence. Secret and confidential matters may be involved. Nixon will probably try to keep this type of activity out of the limelight. If bad publicity is received, he may be upset because it might squelch a deal. Possibly a political competitor would attempt to use these hush-hush negotiations against Nixon (if he's still in power).

During this time, Nixon can be a mystery and lead a life of intrigue. He will probably want to withdraw and have privacy; however, the spotlight can be on him continuously.

If he takes up a hobby, he may become intensely interested in it, only to drop it later.

* * *

The following aspect will start October 29, 1974. The worst peak will be reached November 23, 1976. The discord will start to lift after the peak date. It will be completely out of his chart by February 21, 1978.

ASPECT: *ASC progressed Sesqui-square Pluto progressed and natal*

By progression, this aspect is discordant. There is no aspect in his natal chart between Pluto and his ASC (Ascendant, rising sign); therefore, this aspect is inharmonious.

HOUSES INVOLVED: *The ASC influence* . . . The natal ASC is the 1st house cusp. The progressed ASC is in the 2nd house until September 28, 1976 at which time it will enter the 3rd house.

The Pluto influence . . . The sign Scorpio is on the 3rd house cusp (Pluto is one of the rulers of Scorpio). The natal and progressed Pluto are in the 10th house.

During this time period, Nixon will possibly attract many disturbances and jolts which may bring deviations of a mental and physical nature.

Drastic changes may occur in his personal life and with career. This may be the result of health, scandal, impeachment or because he will lead a new life when his term is up. If you will notice, this aspect will reach the worst peak in November of 1976—election month.

Extreme and dire events can be attracted, accompanied by possible alterations in his plans. There can be a break in his own political party, or a shock with what a member of it concocts against him. Dishonor and disgrace may follow. Pre-existing conditions can be rendered asunder. It's possible that Nixon will have to pave the way for effort along somewhat different lines.

Investigations on illegal activities, which may involve corporations, companies, syndicates, racketeers, or the Mafia, may be contrived by Nixon. Possibly the results will be used against another, held over the person's head for future favors, or the party in question may be publicly exposed. In the first two instances, the individual may be obliged to obey Nixon's bidding. Rebellion may occur, in the third instance, and the criminal in some sneaky manner may implicate Nixon.

Any tapes can now bring drastic results to his image. Scandal and bad publicity may follow. Transcripts of the tapes can now be broadcast to the world. Any recording on tape, at this time, will be most damaging to Nixon (it can be the old tapes now completely out in the open).

It's possible that he's intimidated by crooked people who want him out of office (if he's still in) because he doesn't go along with their desires or principles. However, if he is involved in any crooked operation, Nixon is likely to be caught red-handed. Scandal can result, among other drastic events.

* * *

Nixon may, during this time, attract blackmail, extortion, pay-offs, and all sorts of shady deals. Dubious or ruthless people may try to impede his progress with industry, medical issues, research, nuclear devices, or any area where money, signing agreements and doing good for mankind is concerned (if he's still President).

He is not likely to allow anyone to interfere with his intentions. Nixon probably feels that he must accomplish them at all costs. If he is provoked to any great degree, it's possible that he will be compelled to use devious means to eliminate obstacles.

Any force or pressure employed by Nixon will probably bring agitations, upsets, severe changes and damage his reputation. He should guard against underhanded tactics, exploitation, walking over others and using people for his own selfish gain; although, he will probably assert that it is for universal good.

* * *

NOTE: If he's still President the following may apply:

His efforts will be blocked, if he coerces others to sign or agree to nuclear arms control. He will attract many people now who will probably oppose bills or treaties on atomic energy, tests, experiments or plants; outer space programs and joint participation with foreign lands in any of the preceding areas.

* * *

Agents, aides, representatives or anyone else can create problems for Nixon; especially, if he attempts to control them. If they try to badger or harass him, in return, they will probably receive the same treatment. Nixon may be quite shaken by what is pulled on him. He's not in a cooperative mood now. Anyone who tries to ruin his image, or drastically affect his business, had better step aside!

During this time, he may prefer to make his own rules. It's possible some established codes are broken or violated by Nixon. If he plays a double role, or game, he will possibly be caught and ousted (if he's still President). His power now can be lessened due to scandal, impeachment or illness.

* * *

Two people may approach Nixon, at different intervals, and try to persuade him, in an irreputable manner, to become involved in a particular activity. Later, Nixon can be jolted when he discovers that these two individuals were working with each other against him. Of course, he may be smart enough to play both ends against the middle.

* * *

At committee meetings, others may cause all types of problems for Nixon. Whatever he desires, they'll probably take the opposite view. Groups may try to master, or control him. If they don't succeed, dirty methods to force him out of office (if he's still President) can be employed. He can be depicted as a bad fellow. It's even possible that his brothers will be used in their plots.

A situation may be instigated where he's trapped by a bugging device. Nixon must be extremely careful of what is said to whom and where. There is no privacy for him, during this time. His conversations can be recorded from his car, home or office.

Nixon may be framed, or do the framing. Tapes can be edited. If any eavesdropping, by wiretapping, is brought out publicly, a messy scandal, costing money and ruin, may follow.

A ban on bugging devices may be enforced (if Nixon's still in power). If anyone has hurt him, he's likely to find a way to get even. The person may be placed on his bad list, or a boycott may be in store for the individual.

* * *

The nation might appear as if it's in an upheaval. Rioting and vandalism will possibly occur. Minority, political and big business groups may oppose him. Nixon must be careful of taking sides or collaborating with others in some common cause which may result in a frame-up, or backfire against him.

* * *

Difficulty may be attracted with strikebreakers, picketeers or mediators of labor unions (if he's still in public office). Sit-down strikes and protests may occur outside his home.

If he's still in public office, he could abuse his power as President; especially, when he behaves similar to a dictator. All hell will probably break loose, if he appears on television and demands compulsory codes for the people. They may call Nixon a "fink" and a "meddler" into affairs which don't concern him.

If he brings pressure on people, they are likely to rebel. Hate letters, threats and constant trouble possibly will follow.

* * *

Troublemakers, crowds and deadlines can give Nixon a desire to hibernate. He may feel compelled to be alone so he can read, study and concentrate on the affairs of the moment. *NOTE:* This compulsion, perhaps, will grow stronger as the aspect reaches a peak in his chart.

* * *

Money and Brothers

To earn money may possibly become his obsession. He might have never-satisfying desires toward financial gain. Perhaps, Nixon will say, "There must be a better way to get ahead." As a result, he may stew about it for awhile and then take action.

* * *

Any bad publicity about his brothers, personal life or finances can upset him. If those close to him become involved in any illegality, or are framed, it will bring drastic events into his life.

Care has to be taken while his brothers are on short distance trips or commuting, in case of their being hijacked or shanghaied because burglaries, vandalism and kidnapping can be attracted. If his brothers or other relatives are abducted, ransom money may be paid by Nixon. Currency could be spent as if Nixon was possessed by a demon. Possibly he may turn in the other direction and rebel against kidnappers.

Nixon himself should have extra police protection. Assassination attempts must be closely guarded. He may feel like isolating himself away from mobs and any place where clusters of people are gathered together. Nixon should follow his own inner impressions along these lines.

* * *

The political party that wins the 1976 election will possibly bring a drastic change in Nixon's plans. He will most likely have to make alterations, which may eventually lead him into better avenues of endeavor and can attract new conditions into his life.

Health

There probably will be rumors, gossip and talk about his health during this time period. He can have nervous, tense and jerky movements. If he continues to use force on himself drastic health problems can result.

His insistence and persistence with any idea, or job, can bring constant excitement, strain, stress and tension. His stamina may not be up to par. The well-being of his physical body is likely to be in poor condition.

Pressure and more pressure—he may break under it. Illness can occur while on a short jaunt, or while alone. He tends to be in danger, whether it is through an illness, break-down or someone trying to get rid of him.

74

His colon area may be affected and blocked. Problems can develop with hemorrhoids, hernia, bladder, prostrate gland, bronchial tubes, nervous system, circulation, hives fevers or infections.

* * *

The following aspect starts April 26, 1975. It reaches a peak April 22, 1976. When this peak is reached, the energy will begin to fade; however, the aspect will begin again October 1, 1976. It will reach the last peak October 1, 1977 and then the harmony and discord involved will start to lift. The aspect will be completely out of his chart October 1, 1978.

ASPECT: *Sun progressed Trine Neptune progressed and natal*
By progressions this aspect is harmonious. In his natal chart there is an opposition (which is discordant) between these two planets. The inharmony is greater than the harmony.
HOUSES INVOLVED: *The Sun influence*... The natal Sun is in the 5th house. The progressed Sun is in the 7th house. The sign Leo is on the 12th house cusp (the Sun rules Leo).
The Neptune influence... The natal Neptune is in the 11th house. The sign Pisces is on the 7th house cusp. (Neptune is one of the rulers of Pisces.)

Work
At this time, he will probably do plenty to impress others, receive recognition, and to gain the respect of his associates, partners, pals, loved ones, the public, or anyone who is powerful, influential and wealthy.

Nixon will most likely want others to see how important he is. Praise and a pat on the back may be needed. Credit for his accomplishments will possibly be desired. To be distinguished, and perhaps receive an honor or medal, can be part of his ego trip. It's possible that all of these things will come tumbling down, because others will probably attempt to block Nixon's efforts for the center stage.

He may appear conceited if he brags, lords it over others and tosses his authority around. Perhaps within, he doesn't feel superior, but the desire for approval can be so strong that he compensates with a bossy attitude.

As a result of the foregoing, it's probable that he will attract difficulties with men in power and high political office. Alienation from them can result.

* * *

Nixon may become involved with people of power, heads of state, royalty, influential or wealthy classes and with them, enter into business or secretive undertakings for government or private use.

It's most likely that the meetings he attends, and the arrangements he makes, have an air of mystery surrounding them. Many unexplained factors can possibly be involved. Microfilm of special projects may be discoverd, stolen or given publicity. His enemies may be somehow involved. Nixon should use care that photographs are not taken while conferring secretly with another. The spies he encounters may possibly be his so-called friends.

* * *

If he's still in public office, and Nixon makes promises to the public , his vows or pledges may not be kept. At this time, he will probably see things more favorable than they are, and is not likely to be aware of the impossibility of his idealistic dreams. Because of these actions, his rivals and foes will possibly try to literally tear him down in the public's eyes.

* * *

Nixon may become involved in a project where he desires to aid the poor, or better the living conditions for others. Any undertakings now of this nature will most likely be too idealistic and impractical. Nevertheless, he may still try to tackle them in an exploratory manner. If he does, it's probable that later he will realize that his efforts were wasted because the venture proved worthless, futile and unproductive.

The promises of others must be guarded against because they may be broken, or the truth behind them can be disguised. If discovered, Nixon can be made the fall guy. Deliberate plots to ruin him may occur. He can become lost, like in a fog, not knowing which way to turn, or who to trust (if the preceding occurs).

Court

Nixon may have thought that he was above others and beyond reproach. Disappointed, he can wake up and possibly find a subpoena sitting on his lap. If an arraignment or impeachment takes place, Nixon will be embarrassed and, perhaps, disgraced. Records and documents may be falsified. Data and the facts can be twisted and warped. Surprising discoveries will probably be made.

It's possible that Nixon will disguise topics, problems or questions by making indefinite and unclear remarks. He may withhold information or deviate from the truth to aid his friends. Lies can be told to the public. Also, it's probable that his pals will fabricate everything necessary to help Nixon.

Perhaps, at the last minute, he will be saved. Those who will most likely come through for him are influential, powerful or wealthy men. They may be a member of royalty, head of state, or a close friend.

Friends

A touchiness is now in with his pals. With them, Nixon can show his sentiments and feel any suffering they may have undergone. He's inclined to confide in them—this is likely to be his downfall. Now is *NOT* the time for Nixon to place too much reliance upon their word. If he continues to swear by them, he later may be sorry. His faith in his buddies can create problems; therefore, he should not listen to anyone.

* * *

Possibly attracted are silent partnerships, or business affairs, that are negotiated behind closed doors. Everyone involved may be secretive now, but attention can still be drawn to them and their activities. At this time, nothing will be covered-up for long. Daily discoveries by everyone, including Nixon and the public, may come to light.

* * *

Special privileges or subsidies may be conceded, or promised, to those close to Nixon (if he's still President). If these matters fall through, he will probably back himself by talking big and in superlatives.

* * *

A close buddy may have committed a crime, misdemeanor, or felony. It may now come out in to the open by Nixon's adversaries. A disappointment, in the person, may be felt because he can't possibly conceive that the individual in question could commit such an act.

This experience can be a crude awakening. It can be so shattering that the friendship is broken; and with it, Nixon may desire to be left alone with his disillusionment.

Perhaps, he may say, "These kind of pals are dangerous for me to be around. If I'm in their company, I may be blamed for things I'm not guilty of."

It's now possible that his friends can become his enemies; therefore, it is best for Nixon to be leery of everyone he contacts.

Investments

It's possible that Nixon has exaggerated hopes to make a killing, whether it be with gambling, the stock market or a speculative venture.

However, at this time, the stock market is a gamble for Nixon, and a risky one at that. He should shun the following areas of investment: Gold; oil, gas, petroleum; insecticides; aviation; space capsules; plastics; rubber; foam rubber; pills; patent medicines; microfilm (or any type film) and the motion picture industry.

Friends and brokers can give Nixon wrong advice on the stock market, or he may tell them about a fantastic stock that he has inside information on. Everything, at this time, may turn out as pure nonsense, fall short of what is expected, or peter out entirely.

Nixon should now avoid deals where a number of people share in the profit, such as incorporation. Phony individuals are possibly attracted and someone may try to chisel him out of his just dues. If this happens he may try to use his influence to indict the person.

* * *

At this time, if a pot of gold at the end of the rainbow is promised, Nixon, most likely, will believe it exists. However, because of past disappointments, he will probably be torn back and forth in a terrific conflict about his becoming involved in any schemes. If his imagination is overly-active, and he pictures fantastic sums of money, Nixon may take the person's offer. He shouldn't because the venture will probably turn out to be a mirage.

* * *

The information now given on deals can turn out to be false, or misrepresented. All undertakings which have alluring profits, at this time, should *NOT* be heeded. They may possibly wind up as a hoax, swindle, or may fizzle and fade away into the ethers. Whatever profits are expected, only ten percent is likely to come through.

* * *

At this time, Nixon must take care that others don't lead him astray and make him break a rule, or violate a trust. Dire repercussions can result.

* * *

Most likely, Nixon will be able to enthrall others in his projects, if he uses a gentle persuasive method as his approach. Whenever this slow and irresistible force is employed those who are half-way interested in the undertaking can become so inspired that they will probably jump immediately in, without thinking twice about their action or the venture.

It's most probable that Nixon's thoughts for overnight riches has him towering so high that he can't see the earth below. At this time, he can be gullible enough to try to seize any bubble schemes which may be floating around in

78

the air. The enormous gains, which he believes he will make, will most likely burst wide open like the bubbles he attempts to catch. It will all eventually land on the ground of reality. As a result, Nixon's pocketbook may be a little empty, his head can be swimming, and perhaps he's saying, "I'll never do that again."

* * *

With his close friends, he can make a bet on sporting events, or on who will win the forthcoming election. Nixon can, at this time, attract both gains and losses with any form of gambling.

Dreams, Thoughts, Future
He may have prophetic psychic impressions. They should be heeded. His dreams (both day and night) may increase. Action must be used to bring them to fruition.

* * *

His mysterious demeanor may arouse the curiosity of others. Nixon will probably enjoy this role because of his possible desire to escape from the humdrum of everyday affairs. Also, he may want to be out of the limelight. He tends to now long for peace and harmony.

To satisfy these desires, he may temporarily withdraw from friends and public life. Possibly, a little relaxing, fishing and golfing will please him. At this time, hobbies and pleasures will probably give him a feeling of contentedness. However, Nixon may have an indefinite hankering to do something besides loaf. Perhaps, he will be torn between being retired or having a job of some type.

If he chooses work, Nixon will, most likely, desire a powerful position with status and prestige. If he's a businessman he can possibly have these areas satisfied; also, he would be his own boss.

Nixon might have promised his pals and family that he will retire when he's no longer President. However, someone may come along and offer him a fantastic business proposition. Because he has a tendency now to gain opulence the lazy way, devoid of too much labor, this deal will probably be difficult for him to refuse. If he accepts it he may not realize that he is breaking his words of "retirement" to those near and dear. But the project will probably fall through before his loved ones have time to become too upset.

* * *

When he is no longer in public office, he should, perhaps, be prepared to face being blamed for corruption, lies and all sorts of schemes.

NOTE: These condemnations will possibly come from the new President, an enemy, or a man of power and influence.

Loved Ones

It's possible that Nixon experiences difficulty whenever he's simultaneously with his friends and loved ones. He probably desires to talk to everyone at the same time, but can't hop back and forth across the room; therefore, he may find it easier to keep them entirely separated. This action, he may think, also avoids hurting anyone's feelings because each will have his undivided attention.

* * *

Perhaps, he will have a yen to throw a party and entertain his family or buddies. People in the theatrical profesison may be in the audience or upon the platform. If he has to cancel this or any other social gathering at the last moment, he probably feels that he will disappoint everyone concerned. However, he knows that it can't be helped. Nixon will almost always place business before pleasure. Once he's retired, he may think that he will change, but it's unlikely because the aspect will still be in his chart.

* * *

It will possibly bother him to break a promise to a loved one regarding an outing, holiday, vacation or theatre engagement. If he doesn't keep his word, he most likely will want to someday make it up to everyone. Perhaps, he will succeed.

* * *

It's possible that he expects to be a grandfather. If the daughter has a miscarriage, loses the baby, or has a false pregnancy, he will probably be greatly disappointed. As a grandparent, he will tend to idolize the grandchild and shower the child with loads of love and attention.

* * *

Nixon can, at this time, be in a romantic mood. Perhaps, he may desire to wine and dine Patricia by candlelight, listen to soft melodious music, or hold hands while watching a movie. Toward Pat, he now tends to be warm, sensitive, sympathetic and affectionate. However, it may not always be so easy for him to be this way, but while under this aspect's influence, his finer emotional nature is likely to be aroused; therefore, he can, at last, express these feelings.

80

Nixon will probably have to be careful of giving his wife imaginary attributes which don't exist. At this time, he can be seeing her through the eyes of love, and can be blind to a few of her imperfections. If he awakens from this dream-like state, possibly, he will slowly draw away from her and may become quite detached. It can be similar to a slight parting. It's unlikely that she did anything wrong; but, he will probably have to adjust to this new world of reality. It's possible that it will take a little time for him to become accustomed to it; however, in the final wind-up, he will probably care for her even more than previously.

Health

Illnesses could be attracted to Nixon which are difficult for doctors to diagnose. His system may now lack Vitamins B and E, and he may have an iodine deficiency. The areas possibly affected are the heart and stomach. Whatever his true condition, it's possible that the whole truth will be concealed from the public.

He may now have less liveliness, vivacity, stamina and vitality. His energy can be sapped, but he will probably continue to attempt his various activities with all of his might. It's possible that he needs a rest because he can be emotionally and vitally tired from all of the hectic and negative events which could still be transpiring.

Attracted may be dizzy spells, or the feeling that he has sleeping sickness, or perhaps a blackout occurs after having one drink. If any of these things happen it's most likely that he has poisons in his system.

At this time, he may have difficulty in handling pills, drugs or protein foods. Germs, moist pockets of bacteria and food poisoning can be attracted. Care should be exercised against any strokes, comas, overworking, stress or emotional strain.

* * *

The following aspect starts September 22, 1974. It reaches a peak January 8, 1976 and leaves his chart April 24, 1977.

ASPECT: *Mars progressed Inconjunct ASC natal (rising sign)*

This aspect will be reinforced with another aspect which starts October 22, 1975 and doesn't reach a peak for years.

NOTE: This aspect will never be completely out of his horoscope.

ASPECT: *Mars progressed Parallel ASC natal (rising sign)*

By progression these two aspects are slightly discordant. In his natal chart there is no aspect between Mars and the ASC; therefore, both of these aspects will be inharmonious.

HOUSES INVOLVED: *The Mars influence* . . . The sign Scorpio is on the 3rd house cusp. (Mars is one of the rulers of Scorpio.) The natal Mars is in the 4th house. The progressed Mars is in the 5th house. The sign Aries is on the 8th house cusp. (Mars rules Aries.)

The ASC influence= The natal ASC is the 1st house cusp. The progressed ASC is in the 2nd house until September 28, 1976, at which time it will enter the 3rd house.

Work

To transact business from his home may become more urgent as time passes by. Deals may be pushed through regardless of how the people involved feel about it. This can possibly cause arguments to start. Also, an "I know it all" attitude has to be guarded against.

Whenever people don't agree with him, he may snap at them. Impatient, irritable, nervy, competitive and easily aroused to anger—these traits can possibly become heightened after October 22, 1975. Nixon is inclined to be temperamental and tell people what he thinks. Bad language can predominate conversations. With the passage of time he will possibly become more rushed and hurried to accomplish his set tasks. If Nixon feels held back or others try to slow him down, he will probably be fit to be tied. His attitude of doing everything "right now" can drive him to an even faster pace.

Investments

His gambling spirit can become more apparent after October 22, 1975. However, before that date, he may wager and take a risk of loss or uncertain gain.

Nixon will probably want quick money; therefore, there's a tendency for him to plunge, without thinking things through, into the stock market or real estate. At this time, it's possible that he will *NOT* listen to the advice of others.

He's inclined now to be in and out of business transactions. If he hangs onto his assets, he will probably do better; however, nothing much will come of many of his investments.

Expansion may be thought about, but for it to be effective Nixon will have to push it into action. He will probably have more initiative along these lines after October 22, 1975. From then on, property, dividends, stock, and all of his personal holdings can gradually increase to larger sums.

* * *

Probable areas which he may heedlessly rush into are: Manufacturing; building construction; stock held in ammunition companies; a corporation which deals with deadly weapons or implements used in the destruction or construction of some object.

NOTE: At this time, the preceding matters are not that favorable for him to invest in.

Money, Debts and Taxes

An increase of money may be expected; therefore, Nixon can squander the cash on hand. If the expected legal tender doesn't arrive, he will probably be upset and angry because he spent his other currency.

* * *

If people owe him, he may possibly have an inner struggle to personally collect the money. He could give the job to another whom he feels is more capable. After October 22, 1975, it will be easier for Nixon to go after any legal tender that's rightfully his.

* * *

His debts from September 22, 1974 to October 22, 1975 are likely to be up and down. Nixon can plunge into deeper indebtedness as the years pass by. Especially, after October 22, 1975 when his obligations can slowly build to larger amounts.

* * *

Dissensions, strife and struggle can occur in his private life regarding his money, investments and liabilities. His brothers, daughters or wife may be involved in any quarrels which ensue.

* * *

Care should be taken that he does not become involved in any breeches of the law; especially, if it involves his relatives or real estate transactions. Nixon may help them to acquire a loan through a banking institution, or he may aid them in monetary support in some fashion. If he's still president, he may grant subsidy (in some form) to his brothers.

* * *

A mood may strike him which makes him desirous of expanding his real estate operations, but nothing much may come of his inflated ideas. High assessments and taxes may have something to do with his not taking action. It's possible that Nixon can become quite angry with all of the money he spends in revenue for the government. His taxes will, most likely, continue to cost him plenty; however he will probably endeavor to pay them as quickly as possible.

Health

His strength is, perhaps, not as strong now as it will be after October 22, 1975. His fuel supply can easily be depleted. There's a tendency for Nixon to waste his energy by overdoing everything; however, it's possible that he will perform his duties in spurts and rest in between. With his job (if he has one) there's likely to be too much tension and stress.

* * *

If he exercises, he probably won't use common sense—he possibly will work at it too fast and long. It's probable that his muscles are now weakened. His ankles can be a source of difficulty. Care, when walking, should be taken; otherwise, he may twist his ankle and fall.

* * *

An accident may be attracted, if he's moving too fast, or while riding in a car. Extreme precaution should be taken that no violence occurs at this time.

NOTE: Mars rules ammunition, fires, bombs and other destructive weapons. This aspect is with Mars and the ASC—his physical body.

* * *

Stimulants, like coffee and alcohol, probably don't agree with his system now. Nixon may have trouble digesting protein foods, such as eggs and meats.

* * *

Attracted are possible bruises, rashes, sores, burns, cuts and fevers.

NOTE: If Nixon has a major health problem, this aspect alone is not responsible for it; other aspects are needed (and he has them). To have an operation, he needs a Mars aspect and one to his ASC (the physical body). This particular aspect, which he has in, can attract an operation.

When this aspect first starts, Nixon may begin to think about an operation, but nothing will probably come of these thoughts. However, when the aspect is reinforced with another Mars-Asc aspect, he will possibly, from that date on, have a stronger desire to have an operation. Also, it is more probable to occur after that time period.

Personal Concerns

Quick changes can take place in his private life. When it's time for Nixon to make a move, it will be a fast one. While he's at home, he tends to be quite fidgety. There's possibly a surplus of creative energy goading him to take action. If he doesn't utilize this properly, he may become disturbed with those around him. * * *

His sex drive can be strong. His desires along these lines may possibly become more intense after October 22, 1975. Lovemaking might be rushed because he's in a hurry to do other things.

* * *

The following aspect starts October 9, 1975. The best peak will be reached April 17, 1977. The harmony will start to life after the peak has been reached. It will not leave his chart until October 17, 1978.

ASPECT: *Jupiter progressed Sextile ASC progressed (rising sign)*

By progression, this aspect is harmonious. In his natal chart there is no aspect between Jupiter and the ASC; therefore, this aspect will be completely harmonious.

HOUSES INVOLVED: *The Jupiter influence* . . . The natal and progressed Jupiter are in the 4th house, and the sign Sagittarius is on the 4th house cusp (Jupiter rules Sagittarius). The sign Pisces is on the 7th house cusp (Jupiter is one of the rulers of Pisces).

The ASC influence . . . The natal ASC is the 1st house cusp. The progressed ASC is in the 2nd house until September 28, 1976, at which time it will enter the 3rd house.

Health

His health can improve, although he will probably have to watch gaining weight. Jupiter is the planet giving divine protection; therefore, it's in now, with his physical body, or instead it may work with investments, money, litigations, home and/ or personal affairs. With these matters, he can possibly be saved at the last minute.

Personal Concerns

He will probably appear jovial, happy, carefree, optimistic, unconcerned, unbothered and that everything's fine. His sense of humor now can be great.

Possibly, he's a good sport. Everything can be seen through rose-colored glasses. Most likely, he will now give in to others and go along with their wishes. He tends to be looking forward to everything that life has to offer.

* * *

Increases can occur in his private life. His wife may encourage and inspire confidence in him with matters relating to health, money and business. It's possible that Nixon will feel like dedicating part of his life to her.

* * *

His religious urges can possibly come to the front. This may be more apparent with those close to him; however, they can be noticed whenever he's face to face with the general public. At this time when with strangers for the first time, he is likely to be in a handshaking mood and will possibly crack some jokes.

* * *

Competitors or enemies don't seem to fase him now. If he won a battle, this may be one of the reasons why he's in such a rejoicing mood with everyone whom he contacts.

* * *

If he's a defendant in a law suit, he can possibly, at this time, be saved at the last minute, or if he's suing someone, he is likely to win the case. A large expenditure of money may be paid out now through legal areas.

Associations

He's probably in a "share the wealth" frame of mind. With it, he may attract business partnerships. Those with affluence can be one hundred per cent behind him. Favors may be asked for and granted. Others may feel kindly toward Nixon because he's possibly radiating sunshine and good wishes to everyone.

It's probable that he will now attract more than one partnership. In fact, he can have an abundance of associates in various enterprises. Prospertiy seems to reign. Opportunities for stupendous sums to be made might possibly fly in Nixon's direction. All he has to do is to seize them.

Money and Investments

Favorable chances to make money can come through bankers, financiers, lawyers, or those people who are involved in importing, exporting, shipping, or merchandising. Perhaps, many of his opportunities will come if he listens to the advice of these people, or is in a partnership with them.

* * *

Nixon will probably want to be engaged with people who are honest, ethical, openminded and who will abide by the laws of the land. If he uses these traits and actions, he will be most likely to have new doors open to him, with substantial profits resulting.

* * *

Financial transactions may fascinate him and absorb his personal time. His holdings can now multiply to large amounts.

* * *

He will possibly raise the price on his property. If he wishes to sell, he stands a good chance of expanding his pocketbook to an enormous sum.

If he owns large acreages of land the value of the property may be increased. This can be accomplished through his buying surrounding land, or erecting buildings on the site. After he has done this, he can possibly turn around and sell it to the highest bidder. His ultimate gain will probably be fabulous.

* * *

Enlarging his operations now can prove fortunate, if he applies analytical, rational and deductive reasoning. He has to watch his over confident attitude with speculative ventures. However, whichever way he moves now, he's probably going to gain.

* * *

All of his business undertakings will likely to be stupendously performed. It's possible that petty deals will not interest him, but big money does. He may become involved with shopping malls, centers, plazas or large office structures. Nixon will probably discover that condominium investments can be attractive to his bank account.

* * *

If the rooms in his residence aren't large enough, he may enlarge the whole house, or buy a new one. At this time, a spacious home may be one of his utmost desires. Many rooms may appeal to his sense of freedom. With them, he can move about and feel as free as a bird that's been left loose.

87

Any spending he now does, will possibly be done with a flourish. Nixon may go on a spree and escapade and treat money as if it's going out of style. He will probably go first class, all of the way. Possibly, he may think that it's necessary for him to have the finest, most plush, and swank home he can afford. Perhaps, no cost will be spared on any expensive item, object or clothing that Pat or he desires.

NOTE: Nixon is not likely to spend his money to impress people, or to show off. He probably is in a giving mood. His expenditures can be costly, but he may feel what he obtains in return is well worth the price paid. At this time, it's possible for him to keep money in circulation.

* * *

The following aspect started April 17, 1966. The worst peak will be reached May 17, 1978. The discord will start to lift after the peak date. It will be years before the aspect will leave his horoscope.

ASPECT: *Jupiter progressed Sesqui-square Saturn progressed*

By progression this aspect is discordant. In his natal chart there is no aspect between these two planets; therefore, the aspect will be one of discordancy.

HOUSES INVOLVED: *The Jupiter influence* . . . The natal and progressed Jupiter are in the 4th house, and the sign Sagittarius is on the 4th house cusp (Jupiter rules Sagittarius). The sign Pisces is on the 7th house cusp (Jupiter is one of the rulers of Pisces).

The Saturn influence . . . The sign Capricorn is on the 5th house cusp (Saturn rules Capricorn). The sign Aquarius is on the 6th house cusp (Saturn is one of the rulers of Aquarius). The natal and progressed Saturn are in the 9th house.

NOTE: With this aspect Nixon may appear similar to a Jekyll and Hyde, going from one manner of thinking and acting to an entirely different one. Extremes can be felt; at the moment of each, he may believe entirely in that particular one.

Work

The pressing decisions he must make can create agitations with his employees whenever he swings to and fro (like a pendulum) with opposite answers to his problems. Confusion may seem to reign for everyone concerned. Changes may be in order, but Nixon probably doesn't trust everyone; therefore, difficulties ensue. Worried, he possibly feels the weight of the world on his shoulders. From this frame of mind, he may swing to a sudden alteration of the plans made, and be in a trusting and happy-go-lucky mood. This switching back and forth may jolt those who work under him.

Nixon is likely to be concerned that there will be shortages of raw materials and from out of the clear blue sky—there are. Another day passes and it can appear as if there's a huge supply of goods; therefore, Nixon now may feel confident that there is no shortage. However, a week or so later, he again is likely to be back to his original anxiety about the lack of basic supplies.

* * *

Employees can possibly be taken for granted one moment, and the next he may be afraid he'll lose them. A bonus can be given when he's happy; a cut-back may be thought about when he's blue.

* * *

Work can be serious matter to him. Perhaps, it's a duty he willingly accepts. However, fun (he may think) is a part of living and feeling alive. At times, he might become agitated with himself because he most likely can't combine the two together. He may say, "There must be a better way of doing things."

Foreign Relationships

He will probably always look to other countries for world-wide trade trans-actions which, most likely, will help boost business for everyone. Plans can be made in this direction; however, delays may take place. Trips can be post-poned, but Nixon may enthusiastically think that someday everything will fall into place.

* * *

Ill at ease, with a lack of confidence, Nixon can patiently and slowly negotiate with foreign powers (if he's still President). This may be his old and settled way of taking action. It may not last long because everything is chang-ed whenever he's happy and feels that everything is great. In this mood, he tends to be overly eager, with complete confidence, and may impulsively sign trade agreements with people of other nations. Nixon should guard against waiting too long and losing a deal, or being in such a hurry that he jumps in without thinking things over. *NOTE:* Trade deals can be a part of Nixon's life, whether he's the President or not.

His optimistic thinking can possibly be rendered asunder whenever he is tired. He may feel that it will take forever for his goals to be accomplished. When this mood strikes, he might be fearful that the contracts made will not be maintained or performed, and the others will not keep their part of the bargain. However, with a shipment of goods, his doubts may vanish. Also, he will possibly search for a way to expand all enterprises. Most likely, he now feels that he *CAN* count on others to come sailing through.

* * *

Nixon may possibly believe that all taxes placed on foreign imports should be fair to everyone involved in international trade. However, his judgment, along these lines, can be off-balance. Either he tends to be too restrictive and low, or too lenient and high on the amount levied (If he's still in public office).

Investments

It's possible that he either lacks confidence or has too much of it with real estate, the stock market or any other business transaction. If there's a decrease, he tends to worry, and he can become elated if there's an increase. Any hazards he encounters will possibly continue to be up and down from one moment to the next. A loss can occur in one direction, and a gain in another. One day, he may want to expand his holdings; the next, he's too conservative.

Nixon can be shrewd, calculating and practical for awhile. A little later, a venture can be attracted which will possibly make him throw caution to the wind. He can them become impractical because he probably won't want to count the cost of anything.

* * *

Aggitations with himself can occur if he can't decide whether he should sell what he possesses and buy new land, or *NOT* to dispose of his property, but to purchase additional acreage. His thoughts, along these lines, may possibly be that what he already owns, he's sure of; the other is an uncertainty. A risk, he may think, can be a waste; however, it, also, can be a gain. These two extremes can stir him to a state of frenzy, until he decides to take action, one way or another.

* * *

It's possible that Nixon is planning to enter into a business partnership which will involve international commerce. This is most likely to be after he's out of office. Whenever aggravations occur with foreign nations, perhaps, Nixon is happy that he doesn't have any of his money invested overseas. However, when the affairs abroad are running smoothly, he could be disturbed that his private business ventures in other countries are delayed.

Nixon may partly trust a business partner. In the beginning, he will probably desire to share in the profits; but, once the money starts to roll in, greed and distrust may possibly take over.

The Public

NOTE: The following applies if he's still President of the USA.

When he speaks before the populace, he may one moment talk serious, concerned and admit that there are shortages of goods. Another time, he may smile and say that there's nothing to worry about because there's plenty for everyone.

It's possible that he's afraid of trusting the crowd with too much information; yet, at the same time, Nixon probably realizes that he has to keep the people informed on a few things. He's likely to be constantly trying to weigh what should and should not be told. Either way, he can be in a flurry.

* * *

To be an extrovert before the public, is something that Nixon possibly desires to do. However, there's another side of his nature which will probably make him repress this outgoing instinct.

* * *

Strangers, the public, enemies and rivals can be feared, but a moment later he probably has no qualms about them and possibly feels wonderful in their presence.

Impeachment

For an instant, the people who wish to see him impeached, can possibly upset him. Later, he probably could care less.

One moment he possibly worries that he'll be impeached; the next, he probably feels sure he won't be. If he's impeached, he will most likely be jolted, in a frenzy, humiliated and feel that he was wronged. Whatever changes take place, Nixon should accept them gracefully, because new doors may open which can prove to his ultimate benefit.

Loved Ones

It's possible that Nixon's moods will switch back and forth (with his loved ones). One moment, fun and amusements are desired; the next, it's all a waste of time. He can be too strict and serious with his daughters; later, too lenient and overly cheerful. He can be optimistic or pessimistic with his wife, or she's taken for granted one day; the next, her every move is watched. He feels sexy, only later an indifference can set in.

Health

Nixon may possibly go on and off with a diet, or gain weight only to lose it. If he's served rich creamy sauces, desserts, or foods that contain carbohydrates or fat, he possibly will do either of two things: He may pick at and waste this food in order to be polite, or he will eat it and suffer later. He can discipline himself easily with eating; however, there may be times when he doesn't want to be bothered with this measure. That's when the other extreme is taken—the one of "living it up."

* * *

He may have aches and pains while traveling, but he will probably laugh it off as is nothing was wrong with him.

At this time, Nixon must guard against bad circulation, constriction of the veins and arteries, impurities and acids in the blood stream, and tumors.

* * *

The following aspect started April 17, 1941. It will never reach a peak, and will be in his horoscope his entire life.

ASPECT: *Jupiter progressed Parallel Sun natal*

By progression, this aspect is harmonious. In his natal chart these two planets do not aspect each other; therefore, this aspect is one of complete harmony.

HOUSES INVOLVED: *The Jupiter influence* . . . The natal and progressed Jupiter are in the 4th house, and the sign Sagittarius is on the 4th house cusp (Jupiter rules Sagittarius). The sign Pisces is on the 7th house cusp (Jupiter is one of the rulers of Pisces).

The Sun influence . . . The natal Sun is in the 5th house. The progressed Sun is in the 7th house. The sign Leo is on the 12th house cusp (the Sun rules Leo).

Investments

Nixon can continue to build his real estate or stock market investments to a staggering sum. As they grow, so can his confidence and happiness. As years roll by, he may become quite proud of his business achievements. A profit can somehow always be made. Any losses, or problems, will not hurt him because he will be saved at the last moment.

* * *

His partnerships can gradually increase, and with them, an expansion into bigger and more multi-million dollar transactions. Later, it probably will be

92

easier for him to compromise with others. People are likely to encourage him to invest and can reassure him relative to how much he can gain.

Home Life

It's possible that his residences will eventually acquire more lavish furnishings with each passing year. His homes may have a sense of dignity about them, as well as being ornate. It's probable that an increase of privacy is desired; however, Nixon most likely will always sit in the center stage with all of the spotlights shining on him.

* * *

As time goes by, Nixon will probably be prouder of his wife. Her encouragement and faith in him will probably bring them closer. Laughter can continue to abound between them. It's possible that when he's near her, his energy level is raised.

* * *

Nixon may feel like giving advice and guidance to his daughters or any grandchildren (if he has any of the latter). He most likely wants the best for them all. His family can gradually grow larger through the children and their offspring. Because of them, he will probably become more involved in games and sports. As he grows older, perhaps, he will be more carefree with all of those he holds near and dear. They can possibly help keep him youthful.

* * *

Houseguests, other than family, may increase. Those invited may be in society, politics, powerful positions, religion, show business, or have affluence.

* * *

People will probably always help Nixon be granting him special favors and privileges. If possible, he most likely will try to do the same in return.

* * *

As the oncoming years are approached, his philosophical and religious urges may be elevated to a higher level. Perhaps, he will have a greater tolerance for the views and shortcomings of others.

If he is involved in any legal hassles, people in authoratative positions will probably vouch for him. Lawyers, sponsors, backers, partners, bankers, and eminent people will possibly come rushing to his aid. Most likely he has their respect and devotion.

* * *

Any secret enemy may be discovered. Nixon probably will always be protected from any harm with a foe, rival, or opponent. He may possibly bless and wish them all well!

* * *

The following aspect started April 17, 1973. The worst peak will be reached on June 17, 1985. The discord will start to lift after the peak date. However, the aspect will remain in his chart for years after that peak date.

ASPECT: *Saturn progressed Inconjunct Mars natal*

By progression, and in his natal chart, these two planets make the same aspect. It's a slightly discordant aspect (the Inconjunct).

HOUSES INVOLVED: *The Saturn influence*... The sign Capricorn is on the 5th house cusp (**Saturn rules Capricorn**). The sign Aquarius is on the 6th house cusp (Saturn is one of the rulers of Aquarius). The natal and progressed Saturn are in the 9th house.

The Mars Influence... The sign Scorpio is on the 3rd house cusp (Mars is one of the rulers of Scorpio). The natal Mars is in the 4th house. The progressed Mars is in the 5th house. The sign Aries is on the 8th house cusp (Mars rules Aries).

NOTE: Under this aspect, Nixon can express two opposite types of energy. Two opposite planets are involved in the aspect. Nothing much comes of either one's manifestation, except, perhaps, his becoming upset with himself for behaving as he does while under this aspect.

Work

Nixon can be both patient and impatient with phone conversations, correspondence, people and business. Reports may be hurriedly scanned and, a moment later, picked up again and slowly studied. Nixon can be ready to make a fast move—he stops, thinks about it—and he may be vexed because he restrains himself from taking any action. One moment, he may have a desire to be daring and take wild chances; later, he's probably afraid of going out on the limb.

* * *

Possibly, he desires to tell a person, or the public, what he really thinks. He may repress this urge; however, if he cusses or has any outbursts, it probably won't bring any drastic results. In fact, people are not likely to pay any attention to what he says.

It's probable that if he doesn't talk it's because he may want to hide his innermost feelings. If he lost his cool, he might possibly fear that people will scorn him, or that this action will bring setbacks, losses and upsets to his security.

NOTE: If he takes a risk and does or says something which causes a problem, it's most likely that his diplomacy will save him from further complications.

Those Working Under Him

If his help doesn't give him good service or immediate results, his temper is likely to be short; however, he can control it, if he desires.

Perhaps, his representative to a foreign nation may telephone him to report the latest progress. The news given can possibly cause Nixon to become excited. Immediately, he will probably begin to outline the next step which is to be negotiated. Hours later, or another day, the same person may again call. The news, this time, can possibly be a let down. Snags and bottlenecks might have created minor difficulties. Thus, Nixon's inflated desires have temporarily been deflated.

NOTE: The preceding paragraph may still occur if he's not in office. Instead of being a deal with the United States and another country, it can be a private deal where Nixon has someone working as a go-between.

Foreign Relationships

Nixon tends to be bossy and may desire to push foreign powers into taking quicker action, but he will probably remain humble, quiet, and take his time with negotiations.

Most likely, Nixon will become quite excited whenever arms agreements are discussed. This can possibly be an area that has been preying on his mind for many years. He may desire to rush it through; however, if he doesn't agree on everything, he won't push it until others come to his terms. A delay, in this direction, can possibly depress him.

Nothing much may come of an arms agreement while he is in public office. However, it may draw near. Possibly, he will outline a complete method of approach for the next president. Nixon may believe that this is his "baby" and that he can't let go of until it's been settled.

* * *

Heavy taxes on imported items may attract arguments and dissensions between Nixon and those he negotiates with in foreign lands. Strife of this nature soon fades away, only to repeat at a later date.

NOTE: The preceeding applies if he's still the President of the USA.

* * *

Nixon may become concerned with those countries who are at war with each other. A part of him may desire to leap in; however, he can restrain himself. Perhaps, the latter comes as an aftermath of his past experience along these lines.

However, if he does become involved, a temporary cease-fire may occur, but the war may start again. Perhaps, there will be no real gain, mostly losses. Possibly, this will be the end result either way whether he keeps the USA out of war, or enters into war with other nations.

NOTE: If he's not in power, the preceding two paragraphs, don't apply.

Business

Delays may be attracted with construction work in buildings, trade centers, or his homes; machinery; importing and exporting of raw materials; shipping or receiving ammunition. Nixon may become upset and a little angry or worried that nothing has gone right; but, nothing will probably come of his concerns, outbreaks, or the setbacks.

* * *

The hazards and risks he encounters in business may not amount to much of anything. Nixon will probably use foresight with his real estate investments. Taxes will most likely be uppermost in his mind. He can control his debts, investments and money, if he desires to—out of necessity.

Court

He may desire to go to court to have restrictions lifted, or rules and laws changed. However, unless he initiates his ideas into action, they will be deflated.

* * *

With impeachment matters, Nixon will shun and evade court as long as he legally can. He may appear to ignore statistics. Inside, he's probably not ignoring anything—he's burning up. Most likely, a part of him will want to go to court "right now," so it will no longer be hanging over his head. Another side of him could think that he must be clever, slow and delay everything as long as possible. Perhaps, he believes that his trips will place more attention on foreign transactions, and less on impeachmnent.

96

If Nixon had to appear in court, his anger may not show. Instead, he will probably appear detached, reserved and extremely diplomatic. Nothing much may result after the proceedings are over, if this aspect is the only one in at the time of an impeachment hearing; however, it isn't.

Danger
While traveling on foreign ground, he may possibly feel restricted and in fear of his life. Nixon, most likely, will always need bodyguards and police protection; otherwise, he may never feel completely secure. Any mechanical failures, along the road, can create minor panic waves in Nixon; however, nothing much will probably come of his anxieties.

Health
Long hours of negotiation tends to make him feel impatient that these business matters aren't concluded any sooner. The more drawn out they are, the more weary Nixon becomes.

* * *

He tends to be susceptible to colds or throat problems, mainly when he's fatigued and worried.

* * *

His system may contain too many acids, especially if he drinks stimulants (coffee and alcoholic beverages). He could have a protein deficiency because that which is partaken is possibly not assimilated.

* * *

Operations can be delayed, partly due to a fear of death, but mainly because he doesn't want to miss any necessary work or an emergency may possibly arise. Nixon dislikes wasting his time with illness.

He should guard against: Sluggishness due to constipation problems, falls, assassination attempts.

* * *

The following aspect starts October 14, 1975. The worst peak will be reached in June of 1977. The discord will start to lift after the peak has been reached. The aspect will leave his chart by the end of 1978.

ASPECT: *Venus progressed Square Uranus progressed*

By progression this is a discordant aspect. In the natal chart these two planets are in a Semi-sextile aspect. A Semi-sextile is slightly harmonious; a Square is highly discordant; therefore, this aspect is one of great inharmony.

HOUSES INVOLVED: *The Venus influence*... The sign Libra is on the 2nd house cusp (Venus rules Libra). The natal Venus is in the 6th house. The progressed Venus is in the 8th house. The sign Taurus is on the 9th house cusp (Venus rules Taurus).

The Uranus influence... The natal and progressed Uranus is in the 5th house. The sign Aquarius is on the 6th house cusp. (Uranus is one of the rulers of Aquarius.)

NOTE: This aspect can bring a termination of something—a job, love, etc. Whatever it is, it may be sudden and, perhaps, shocking!

Work

At this time, anything is likely to happen. One event after another may occur; they are all surprising. With them, Nixon's hands can be full.

NOTE: The following events may occur whether he's President or not.

Perhaps, a nationwide strike will take place, which turns everyone and everything upside down. Power shortages, with blackouts, may create utter chaos when a business or industrial concern has to close its doors. Billions of dollars can be lost. Nixon, and others, may possibly have some real financial problems.

How will Richard Nixon feel during this time period? Obstacles may occur with others because they might not accept his views. His ideas tend to be new and too far ahead of the times. People will try to block him.

These actions against him, probably won't stop Nixon. His own rules can be devised. Anything that displeases him may be cast aside; this includes people.

His aspirations and goals can be turned topsy-turvy. There may be an uncontrollable and rendering asunder of almost everything he touches. New projects in research, or other areas, may fail to materialize at the concluding stage.

* * *

Attracted are constant disruptions, changes and unexpected reversals. It seems that whatever he plans to do in one direction, goes in an extreme opposite. Most of Nixon's ordeals, dilemmas and problems at this time will probably come through people. There is no way for him to control the unexpected actions of others. However, he can try to handle the events constructively; although it probably will not be easy to do. At this time, he should guard against taking the easy way out.

* * *

Whenever he addresses people publicly, most likely, he will not be well received because of his extreme views and beliefs, or if he expressed radical political convictions. Any erratic behavior now will probably go against him.

* * *

He can now attract controversy, from all sides. In a jiffy, his designs or proposals can be tossed out the window. If he is still in office, an unbelievable (to Nixon) upheaval may occur. Possibly, this may involve his trying to have a new law passed which may concern taxes, social security, unemployment insurance; new projects or tests.

* * *

A shocking change may occur in the administrative department of the United States. If Nixon's still in office, he can attract mutiny with his staff. The person causing the problem may be the one he least expects. The individual can be someone who Nixon has gone out of his way to help. This may be quite a jolt for Richard.

* * *

A homosexual (friend, acquaintance, employee, or someone in a foreign country) may make a sexual advance in Nixon's direction. If this occurs, he will be in complete shock! Perhaps, it will be a person who he never suspected of being that way. If he's still President, and the person is an aide of his, he will probably clean-up the government. If it's a pal, the friendship may be broken. If it's the help, the individual, most likely, will be fired.

* * *

Nixon's working atmosphere can be tense now. The service and aid he receives from others may be very upsetting. Jobs can be left unfinished, or not performed properly, or the place of business may be disorganized, or everything may be in a state of confusion.

People can be careless, which may result in mishaps, hazards, accidents or a verbal fall-out. The wage earners, he employs, can possibly demand a raise in pay. If Nixon doesn't comply, they may go on a strike, or walk off the job. At this time, he should be prepared for all contingencies.

* * *

If he's still President, the following may possibly occur: Unexpectedly, like a bolt of lightning from out of the blue, some members of his staff may quit, or be fired. He may have trouble with replacing them; perhaps, no one will want any of the jobs offered. *NOTE:* If he is out of office, at this time, the preceding paragraph may still be effective.

* * *

If he's still in power, perhaps, someone will try to overthrow him, or have a new law passed and put into effect which may cause harm to his image. Whatever happens, Nixon will likely to be the one blamed for all foul play. Strain and stress with stormy dissensions may possibly follow. Barriers will probably be placed in Nixon's pathway. He may blow his stack with the events which follow: If he's still in office, he can be fired or impeached! His whole life can be completely changed. He will probably be dumbfounded by whatever takes place. If he is impeached, the person causing it will most likely be a member of his staff—someone he trusted.

* * *

It's possible that his health will now break down. If this occurs (and he's still President), he may resign, or others may discover a legal maneuver to have him ousted.

* * *

NOTE: A part of the time that this aspect is in Nixon's chart, he will have completed his term as President, if he isn't fired or impeached beforehand, or hasn't resigned.

This aspect can work as a problem in many of the areas, already mentioned, or those which will be referred to later. Once he is no longer President of the United States, the aspect will *STILL be in his chart*. Therefore, obstacles, in other directions, can be attracted.

* * *

Perhaps, a new and completely different type of job may come flying in Nixon's direction. He should allow it to fly right on by because it probably will not last and, if he takes it, it's likely to bring many headaches and crazy problems.

* * *

In 1977, temporary and part-time work will be the best bet for Nixon, if he desires an occupation. However, at this time, he can't count on much of anything. Whatever he does, he can expect cancellations, disruptions and money problems.

Foreign Relationships
If he's still serving the country, negotiations with other lands may be cancelled before, or during, a session. Nixon's efforts at harmony may be

blocked by a fellow-worker, aide, or foreign power. Several other reasons for any change in plans may be: A strike, revolution, new government, impeachment, a disaster area which needs emergency care, or perhaps, something else from out of left field!

Importing, exporting, or travel which involves other countries may be impeded by a strike. Research projects with people overseas can, at this time, be rejected. Others may not buy any new, inventive or original ideas or objects and create astounding (to Nixon) problems in these areas.

* * *

Money can be a hassle. People may not have it to spend. The dollar could possibly be devaluated lower. Cash flowing in and out of the states may be spot-checked by the Internal Revenue Service, or customs people. Perhaps, a new law will be passed in the direction of the latter. If so, this will possibly be a big problem and the public is likely to rebel and cry for "changes" to be made. This currency check could be bad for those depositors of Swiss banks. The people who place their money in them would possibly revolt if their money leaving the country had to be declared. Perhaps, a situation like this could upset Nixon (especially if he has money in foreign banks).

New deals with taxes which concern those abroad may create a barrier between the U.S. and another country. If this be the case, Nixon's in for a rough time (if he's still in power).

* * *

If, while serving the country as President, he receives an unusual luxury gift from a person in a foreign land, Nixon may desire to keep it after he leaves office. He might possibly attempt to change the law in this direction. If this occurs problems may ensue. A big stink can be raised. If he vanishes with the jewels, or someone else does, all hell will break loose! Naturally, for the latter action, Nixon will be blamed.

* * *

NOTE: The following applies if he's still President:
A gift to a foreign ruler can create an uproar if the present was given personally by Nixon, or in behalf of the United States government. Shocking, (to Nixon) and unreal events, can possibly follow.

* * *

Any social gathering involving Nixon can be cancelled suddenly. The reason may be unexpected business deals, wars, riots, blackouts, strikes, problems with the help (cooks, waiters, etc.), someone becomes ill, or a sudden death occurs.

* * *

Money

If Nixon's still President, he should be careful that the taxpayer's finances don't go down the drain in needless disbursements with luxury items for self, employees, or as presents to those in power overseas. The public will probably rebel at any thoughtless outlay of their money.

At this time, he possibly is not rational in handling other people's legal tender. Crazy things may be done with currency. Even his own money can suddenly be spent on out-of-the-ordinary items.

* * *

Emergencies may pop up with someone (daughter, loved one, companion) who needs instant cash. Nixon might possibly have to loan his money out quickly. By doing this, his business plans may be radically changed, or financial reversals may take place.

* * *

Nixon's pocketbook may be drained with so many debts. Difficulty, at this time, can be in store for him because of the possible necessity of borrowing so much money to take care of the crucial events which might have transpired.

* * *

The income tax people can possibly decide to spotcheck his taxes. An accountant or auditor might have neglected an important item or figure regarding Nixon's loans, debts, stock, dividends or interest payments.

The Internal Revenue Service may catch the error and Nixon can be caught in a mess of red tape and legalities. He may have to appear in court and testify against the person who handled his taxes. The individual may shock Nixon if he leaves Richard holding the bag! The fines and penalties which are most likely to follow, will probably dumbfound him.

Investments

If his account in the stock market has been manipulated by his broker, when Nixon hears the news about it, he will probably be stunned. At this time, he has to be careful of brokers, hot tips, and all speculative ventures. Gambling of any form can now prove hazardous for him.

It's possible that Nixon has money invested in a company which declares bankruptcy. It may be a company that a close acquaintance owns, but the person hasn't informed Nixon of the latest developments. If he had, it's possible that Richard could have pulled out before any disaster had occurred.

NOTE: It's possible that Richard Nixon will declare bankruptcy under this aspect.

* * *

The stock market can crash, or may have a new look. Perhaps, there is a different approach to buying, selling and investing, in general. Computers can possibly be used. The whole system and procedure may be radically changed. This could upset Nixon because he's accustomed to the old way; however, he may be all for it because it possibly eliminates a broker. With this in mind, he can save commission fees and do his "own thing."

* * *

Losses in the stock market, at this time, will possibly be with the following: Computers, electronics, loudspeakers, microphones; items which use wiring, electrical gadgets or equipment (appliances, tools, electric guitars, etc.); modern mechanical devices; automobiles; inventions, fads, novelties; the garment industry; textiles; jewelry; wigs; cosmetics; or a company on the exchange who is involved with research; scientific matters; new developments, plants, products, processes, or information areas.

Health

At this time, he should take extra care that his own health, and those he loves, is in tip-top condition. If Nixon doesn't feel good, he will still tend to go out of his way and please everyone else.

* * *

He tends to be high-strung, tense, on edge, jumpy, and uncoordinated. Sudden health problems may occur with his veins. His feet can be a problem, and walking a difficulty. His circulation may be poor. There is a possiblity of some type of paralysis or stroke. This is a serious and grave time for his health—probably the most dangerous period coming.

* * *

He may lose large quantites of hair. Skin blemishes (from eating too many sweets or carbohydrates) can occur.

Close Relationships

Social affairs may be a source of difficulty now. People may slight him, or be impolite; or the reverse—they can flatter, tempt and then drop him, or cause some unusual problem later.

* * *

Surprises may occur with his daughters. Perhaps one will write a book about him, join the women's lib, or divorce her husband, disappear on purpose, decide to raise funds for the needy, take a radical view, become pregnant, lose a baby, or anything else of an unusual or unexpected nature.

* * *

Estrangements, reconciliations, breaks or unanticipated partings may occur with his wife. There is no warning about what can possibly take place. Nixon will probably be stunned or hurt, because of it. Entertainments, fun, pleasure and business may be cancelled or put aside. He may possibly feel that one part of his life is over and a new one is opening up.

* * *

If an old love is out of his life, a new one may appear; or if he's still married, it's possible that he may attend a social function and meet a woman who will probably fascinate him.

This person may glance at him adoringly. He might be enchanted and completely in awe of her. If he has a romance with her, it probably will not last.

She may cost him plenty. Business can be disrupted for her. Trips may be cancelled. His whole life can be changed. She may stimulate his mind with unusual subjects, such as the occult area.

Obstacles may be in the way of their relationship. She, or he, may be married. Perhaps, she will stay away from him, or disappear. Unusual circumstances exist and the ending may flabbergast him.

He should take care of being misguided or manipulated by this person (or anyone else). If they break up, a replacement, equally fascinating may enter into his life. Anyone new in his life will probably not last, at this time.

* * *

The following aspect has always been in Nixon's chart. A peak will never be reached. The aspect will be in for the remainder of his life.

ASPECT: Pluto progressed Parallel Saturn natal

This aspect was reinforced with additional energy when another type aspect started with the same two planets. The next aspect started April 17, 1920. It is applying toward a peak, but never reaches one because it starts to retrograde. It will be in for many years.

104

ASPECT: *Pluto progressed Semi-sextile Saturn natal*

By progression the Parallel aspect is slightly discordant because Saturn is involved; the Semi-sextile, by progression, is slightly harmonious. In the natal chart there is a Semi-sextile aspect between these two planets; therefore, this is a negative and positive influence—some harmony, some inharmony. the aspect was mostly discordant up until April 17, 1920, at which time some harmony came in when the progressed Semi-sextile started.

HOUSES INVOLVED: *The Pluto influence*... The sign Scorpio is on the 3rd house cusp (Pluto is one of the rulers of Scorpio.) The natal and progressed Pluto are in the 10th house.

The Saturn influence... The sign Capricorn is on the 5th house cusp (Saturn rules Capricorn). The sign Aquarius is on the 6th house cusp. (Saturn is one of the rulers of Aquarius.) The natal and progressed Saturn are in the 9th house.

Safety

Secret service protection will probably always be needed. On purpose, he may have spies in his employ, because with them, Nixon has a good chance to know who is and who isn't against him. If anyone appears suspicious, and Nixon has his doubts about that individual, he probably will have the person investigated.

Court

If Nixon stands before a group of people, he will most likely stick to his beliefs and his decision. No jury, judge, or political party can possibly sway him to make any changes; however, he will probably worry about the results his actions will bring.

Work

Organized corporations may try to harass or pressure him to grant favors to them (while he's still in office). Nixon will possibly try to be as cooperative as possible. If they attempt a bribery, or become dictative, that probably will be the end of their relationship.

It's possible that Nixon will be placed on the spot or in a bad situation with these people. If this happens, he will discover an escape route, or if necessary, expose them. He may prefer to be secretive with these matters; otherwise, he can possibly attract more problems with the public and possibly courts.

* * *

Labor union disputes are most likely taken seriously. If he's still in public office, he will probably patiently weigh all the pros and cons before stepping into any mediations. If he does interfere, he should be careful of making strict, compulsory codes for others to follow.

If he's still President, Nixon may take action and enforce his own rules to quiet things down if: The public rebels against law and control; the mobs and masses are out of hand. This can occur with strikers, picketeers; vandalism, riots or kidnappings.

* * *

His scheduled broadcasts are probably well thought-out and planned to a minute detail. Nixon will possibly try to make the crowds have confidence in him and the situations he is informing them about.

* * *

For many years, he might have done intensive thinking toward job opportunities for the underprivileged, handicapped, poor, or any minority group. If he is to develop these areas into something worthwhile, he will have to apply initiative. Most likely overnight results will not happen.

Conservation of natural resources has possibly been a realm that has become more important to him. It's probable that he will demand, in a nice manner, that research be employed with chemicals. Nixon may believe that the basic materials can be saved if a chemical can reproduce the same effect. Nixon will most likely cooperate with people interested in this field and he can be involved with a team of scientists, huge industrial concerns, or any large group involved in ecology.

* * *

If he limits the public with the buying of certain scarce goods, many will probably oppose him; however, the final results will be in his favor. His main concern now can be a shortage of supplies, which could create a panic (if he's still President).

Foreign Relationships

He may sense that his mission in life (the reason for his existence) is to bring all people together and to save the world by uniting peace and industry.

* * *

It's likely that his overseas trips will always be carefully planned.

While he's in foreign lands on business, Nixon can patiently and enjoyably watch the marching of those in uniform. The clockwork precision with the soldiers in unison can possibly appeal to him.

Tourism, sporting events and world affairs may be part of Nixon's international unity plan to bring aid and money to the United States and other countries. He may possibly feel that if everyone will cooperate they all stand a good chance to make money; with this in mind, perhaps he may think that peace will be easier to achieve.

While traveling and in public office, Nixon will most likely always be in close touch with his staff, or associates. Constant communication is probably a must. All phone calls are probably a part of the daily schedule. His duty, he may possibly feel, is to know the latest developments; therefore, everyone concerned will have to abide by his strict rules along these lines.

Nixon can deal easily with people in communistic countries. He has an inner sense guiding him so he can reach them in a beneficial manner. Their interests are, most likely, known to him and he will probably utilize this knowledge.

Before Nixon becomes involved in a particular overseas trade or transaction, he probably will read and study numerous reports. Every factor probably will be carefully scrutinized. Most likely uppermost in his mind will be how the masses and industry can possibly benefit.

All negotiations will probably take time. One by one treaties and agreements can be signed (if he's still the President). Once a document has Nixon's signature, he does not renege. Perhaps, it's because to him commitments are serious matters that are not to be tampered with, nor broken.

With the administration of goods to foreign countries, Nixon can be thrifty. In these areas, he will, most likely, reject any extravagant and useless spending. A budget can be made with an itemized proportional plan for spending. Once resources are allocated Nixon is probably ready for action (if he's still the President).

While being a guest abroad, Nixon can easily comply and submit to the code or protocol of those in power. However, he probably doesn't want any of them to force him into an area which doesn't appeal to him. The matters that have been on his mind for a long time will, most likely, be preferable to accomplish before he becomes involved in new fields (if he's still the President).

* * *

The future of children and young people all over the universe, he may seriously consider as his responsibility. Possibly, Nixon desires to protect and aid them. Their education can be extremely important to him.

With the passing of time, Nixon may become more involved in student exchange programs. Other more important items on the agenda may have pushed this one temporarily into the background; nonetheless he probably hasn't forgotten about it.

* * *

Any negotiations he attempts for the betterment of the world with foreign powers may possibly never bring him the credit he actually deserves. The pat on the back will probably go to others. However, Nixon's efforts on behalf of all countries will slowly develop, grow, and bear fruit when another man is President of the United States. His inner thoughts may possibly be that he, at least, initiated many good deeds.

Investments

Nixon can buy, in volume, at a low price and may wind up ahead—with the following stock: Commodities, such as hay, grain, wheat, barley, rye, oats, millet, soybeans, coal, timber, lumber, rocks, ores, minerals, utilities; raw materials; cheap items; chemicals; microwave equipment; x-rays, nuclear energy, fuel and power plants; medicine; tape recorders; transistors; radio; television areas.

* * *

Perhaps, he will always be interested in real estate investment, especially large parcels of land that he can hold on to and sell at a later date, or subdivide. Other good areas for Nixon to invest in are housing projects and prefabricated homes.

* * *

The following aspect will start September 21, 1976. This aspect will never reach a peak. It will be in his chart for the remainder of his life.

ASPECT: *Saturn progressed Inconjunct Mercury natal*

By progression, and in his natal chart, there is an Inconjunct aspect between these two planets; therefore, the aspect will be slightly discordant.

HOUSES INVOLVED: *The Saturn influence* . . . The sign Capricorn is on the 5th house cusp. (Saturn rules Capricorn.) The sign Aquarius is on the 6th house cusp. (Saturn is one of the rulers of Aquarius.) The natal and progressed Saturn are in the 9th house.

The Mercury influence . . . The sign Virgo is on the 1st house cusp. (Mercury rules Virgo.) The natal Mercury is in the 4th house. The progressed Mercury is in the 7th house. The sign Gemini is on the 10th house cusp. (Mercury rules Gemini.)

Home Life

From September 21, 1976 and on, Nixon may be fussy and difficult to get along with because of guilt, letdowns and regrets. The areas he possibly feels this way about may be with work, publicity, foreign deals, or court cases. One moment he can be slightly happy; the next, unhappy.

If he has indefinite plans for the future mental restlessness can result. Uncertainty, boredom and a lack of interest may possibly make him want to stay home and mope.

* * *

There's a tendency now for him to be unsocial, seclusive and not in a mood to entertain others. If he does have guests over, he may not enjoy himself. Perhaps, he doesn't trust people. His suspicions can now be easily aroused. He may not utter a word because he may believe that, "Silence is golden."

There's a possibility of misunderstandings between Nixon and his servants, or any employees. He could worry that they will gossip or write about him. At this time, nothing much comes of his fears.

* * *

Errors and misapplications made by his help may possibly disturb him. Once corrected, his satisfaction will probably show. He can waste his time needlessly now by dwelling too long on unimportant problems. His mind seems to be clogged with too many preoccupations; therefore, it can be difficult for him to render a decision. He should be cautious now and not make any unwise or ill-considered changes. However, if he does, it won't likely be anything too drastic.

* * *

There may be shortages of food, paper, natural resources, raw materials or basic supplies. Possibly, Nixon worries about them all and wishes he could do something about it.

Nixon may have a personal loss, or feel apprehensive that he will have one. If he lost a person, he may grieve, or miss the individual. If he lost a residence, he can miss it. If he lost a limb, or part of the body, he would be upset. Whatever occurs could make him feel guilty and depressed; however, nothing much comes of the worry he undergoes with this aspect.

* * *

Nixon can feel indifferent about lovemaking, or possibly worry that he's impotent. He may have a notion that his wife will divorce or leave him. His speech can be repressed with loved ones, but nothing really comes of his anxieties.

Health

His physical body may be tired and weary with many slight aches and pains. One moment he may be rather talktative; the next, grim and quiet. A lack of work, and his mind or nerves being overtaxed can create fatigue.

* * *

Negative thinking can easily creep in because he's probably too tired to fight it off. Earlier health difficulties may have deprived him of work. At this time, if he's ill, he may possibly feel that there is no physical improvement in sight; especially, if he's confined.

* * *

He may have a restricted diet—bland and uninteresting. A loss of weight can possibly occur. Nixon may attract trouble with elimination, bowels, constipation—the colon area. Also, throat problems. His nervous system can be somewhat impaired. Circulation may not be what it should. Constrictions in the veins should be closely watched.

It's possible that he has a calcium and mineral deficiency because he has difficulty in assimilating foods which contain them.

Work

Nixon may have an idea that he should write a book. It's possible that he will want others to understand him better and to clarify the events which transpired in his last years as President of the United States.

Any writing or speaking he attempts now may be restricted. He tends to be too evasive about many areas; in fact, plenty will, most likely, be omitted if he wrote anything at this time. Nixon will probably stall, if he had to grant an interview with a reporter. It's just as well he does, because at this time he could be misquoted or misconstrued. If this occurs, it probably won't amount to anything that will disturb him.

Publicity

If anyone gossips, or makes statements against him, Nixon can possibly become quite negative when it's discovered. Any disgrace to his name is likely to upset him. Bad publicity can make him desire to retreat more from the limelight.

Foreign Relationships

Travel to foreign lands can cause him to worry because he could possibly think that he will not be treated as nice now as he was when he was President. Fear of physical harm may make him delay any trips.

If he does travel, he may possibly have some restrictions. Tight security will probably be needed. Customs can cause him a headache. People may try to impose upon him. Minor difficulties may ensue, but nothing that he'll lose any sleep over.

Court

Cases could have been hanging in the air for some time, or possibly Nixon is apprehensive that someone will take him to court. He's probably not in the mood now to appear before any judge; therefore, he will probably take measures to evade and delay any legal matter. If he is involved in any lawsuit, he will possible settle out of court. At this time, he probably doesn't feel like talking or explaining anything to anyone.

* * *

The MC (Media Coeli, Midheaven, 10th house cusp) in Nixon's chart, for many years, has been in the sign Leo and progressed into the 11th house of friends.

The MC in Leo implies that Nixon probably needs attention and publicity from friends. Possibly attracted into his life are important, eminent, wealthy, powerful and famous celebrities. These people can enter his life through his career and position (MC progressed into 11th house and ruling 10th house). Nixon's friends and acquaintances have an influence that varies. Some years they will be a good influence, and others, a detriment. (This is dependent upon the progressed aspects to the MC.)

On February 26, 1976, the progressed MC will leave his 11th house of friends and enter into his 12th house. This will possibly bring many changes in Nixon's way of living and thinking.

His pals and acquaintances probably will not be as important to him as in the past. In fact, it's probable that he won't want to be with them that much anymore.

With the progressed MC in the 12th house, Nixon can desire the limelight less. He may withdraw, be in solitude and seclusion. His business will probably be done more now behind closed doors than it was before. This includes private alliances and negotiations. Secretiveness may be more important now than in the past. Perhaps, his life will be more of a mystery.

He can possibly become active in research areas. Disappointments may occur easily with any work or project. Publicity can still be attracted, but not as much as prior to February 26, 1976.

It's possible that he may, in some way, be confined or restricted.

NOTE: His MC progressed in the 12th house can become involved in various areas, or lead a life of solitude. The 12th house also rules places of confinement such as hospitals, jails and institutions. Anyone of these areas can be activited while the MC makes a discordant aspect to another planet.

* * *

The ASC (Ascendant, rising sign, 1st house cusp) in Nixon's chart for many years, has been in the sign Scorpio and progressed into the second house of money and personal possessions.

The ASC in Scorpio implies that he has strong likes and dislikes. Also, it can possibly make him have a persistent force that he must accomplish all of his aims which can be turned toward amassing huge amounts of personal holdings. Perhaps, Nixon's burning desire for money is so he can compulsively spend it.

With the ASC in Scorpio, he isn't likely to forget any hurts. He can be resourceful, secretive and, perhaps, sexy.

On September 28, 1976, the progressed ASC will leave his 2nd house of money and enter into his 3rd house. This will possibly create a new attitude and attract many different things into his life.

NOTE: The main difference is the Scorpio attitude now will be directed toward other areas and away from financial ones.

With the progressed ASC in the 3rd house, possibly, there will be less thinking about money and personal possessions. The new emphasis will be chiefly on communications, transportation, education, mental activities and the brothers. He will feel strongly compelled to read, learn, write, travel or become involved in business with any of these activities.

PART THREE

Nixon's Monthly Moon Aspects

The Moon moves faster than the other planets. On June 29, 1974, the Moon entered into the ninth house of Nixon's horoscope. It will be in this location until January 15, 1977.

THE MOON'S INFLUENCE

During this time period, the emphasis will be on court (impeachment or lawsuits), foreign relationships, countries, trade, commerce, or broadcasting his opinions publicly (through television and radio).

The Moon rules publicity, the general classes of people, the mood he is in every month and his subconscious thoughts and emotional reactions. Also, it rules the way the public will react to his actions and words. Each month, these areas will fluctuate between being favorable and unfavorable.

If Nixon had to go to court and stand trial, during this time, it depends upon the Moon aspects for the decision of the judge and jury. During harmonious aspects, he will be fortunate; during discordant aspects, he will be unfortunate.

In Part Three, the houses involved with the Moon's influence are numbers 6, 9 and 11. The natal Moon is in the 6th house. The progressed Moon is in the 9th house until January 15, 1977 at which time it will enter into the 10th house. The sign Cancer is on the 11th house cusp. (The Moon rules Cancer.)

* * *

The following aspect started in July 1974. It reaches a peak November 15, 1974 and leaves his chart in February 1975.

ASPECT: *Moon progressed Parallel Neptune (natal and progressed)*

By progression this is a neutral aspect. In his natal chart there is no aspect between these two planets. *NOTE:* Discord is added to the neutral aspect because when Neptune is involved only 10% can be believed of what is said or promised, or what one desires to accomplish. However, the influence can be harmonious and discordant, dependent upon how Nixon utilizes it.

HOUSES INVOLVED: See page 113 for the Moon's influence. The natal Neptune is in the 11th house. The sign Pisces is on the 7th house cusp. (Neptune is one of the rulers of Pisces.)

Events which are unexplainable may be attracted. His reaction tends to be secretive, detached, polite and he most likely will cover-up all accusations with a mirage of words. Care must be used, so he's not caught in a web of pretense.

Health

Nixon can become lazy. He may feel as if he has sleeping sickness. More rest than normal is possibly required. His energy may be blocked because he's thinking about other things—like the day he can retire and withdraw from public life.

His imagination may magnify his condition as being worse off than he actually is.

Doctors will probably have a difficult time diagnosing his case. Perhaps the public will be told that he's fine; however, fibs about illness may be flying in the air.

Psychic

During this time, he most likely has good ESP ability. Nixon may have many varied psychic experiences and hunches. This can be in relation to impeachment, foreign nations, and with those who work under him. His dreams tend to be more vivid now. Nixon should pay some attention to them.

Wife

One of his aims now may be to escape from the public and to be with his wife. His feelings tend to be inclined toward candlelight, being romantic by wining and dining in places where soft music plays in the background.

He can be up on cloud nine with his mate, and think that she's tops. In conversing with her, many words will probably be left unsaid. His thoughts can be unclear and a little hazy now, because subconsciously he's possibly dwelling on impeachment, his job, resignation, enemies, travel and foreign countries.

A gradual, unintentional withdrawing from Patricia may occur. His mood with her for the moment can be whimsical, and he could see her in a different light as November 1974 approaches.

She may be implicated, in a distant way, with a court hearing. Publicity can follow. She should remain quiet, if interviewed.

Friends

He can promote his buddies so they will be interested in his projects. Nixon may possibly become quite engrossed in various business affairs (mainly those in other lands). His pals can be given some tips for investments, or others in foreign countries may include him in on some inside information.

Fast gains are probably desired. With that in mind, Nixon has to guard against being taken, or having a deal misrepresented. Some of the promising things can fall by the wayside. However, he may not invest in any of the hot tips, but he may pass it along to a pal who will. This can possibly infringe upon the friendship.

* * *

Plans can be made for vacations, outings, relaxations (like fishing), but Nixon may have to renege because of a trip to a foreign land. Those disappointed may be his favorite cronies or loved ones.

* * *

His friends can lie, their words may be distorted, twisted and warped. The type of people who are most prone to this are in the theatrical profession, aviation field or promoters.

* * *

Many of his business affairs can be camouflaged. The truth possibly is not being told. Phony deals may take place. A trap can be laid. Nixon may fall right in. Perhaps his so-called buddy will turn out to be an enemy.

* * *

A show business personality who's a friend can upset him if this person receives bad publicity while in a foreign country. This pal may call on him for some help. Nixon may want to come to the individual's rescue, but he should take care that he isn't implicated now in other people's problems.

Those Who Work Under Him

The working environment can have an air of intrigue. It's possible that spies are around where Nixon least expects them. People will probably be afraid to say much. Intense situations may build—so can lies. Soon perhaps no one will know who's telling the truth.

* * *

Most likely he will not receive the good service he expects. Procrastinations may be partly involved. Also, shiftless employees may try to con him. Perhaps Nixon's representative (to a foreign nation) will not fulfill all of Nixon's expectations. It's possible that Nixon doesn't see the person objectively.

* * *

Drama can ensue while discussions take place with members of his staff (if he's still President). Perhaps a subordinate is promised a better position, or granted a favor. Employees can now be easily influenced; however, Nixon

115

must guard against deception. His dependence upon others may now bring disappointments.

* * *

If an aid, or friend, appears in court to testify for or against Nixon, lies may be told, records may disappear or be falsified.

The press will probably blow everything out of proportion. Nixon's reaction may be vague, elusive and mysterious. It's possible that his mind may actually go blank when reporters ask him certain questions.

If Nixon had to stand trial, care should be taken not to twist the truth, because he may wind up trapped in a fib. He tends to be in a fog during this time, and may not realize what he has stated. As a result of whatever transpires, he most likely won't believe the current events.

Foreign Relationships

Idealism can be in. Perhaps Nixon wants better conditions for the USA and other countries. There's a tendency for him to be impractical.

* * *

His promotional schemes for everyone to become rich overnight may not be fully realized. Oil, gas and petroleum transactions will possibly be a few of the reasons for his visits to other countries.

He will most likely have high hopes that 100% of his propositions will be accepted. Disappointments may follow because only 10% can be counted on to come through. Many transactions will probably fall by the wayside.

* * *

Later Nixon has to guard against making promises to foreigners and the public which he may break. His compassion for those in foreign lands can possibly be strong—sympathy may go to them. He must be careful that his emotions don't run away with him now. It's probable that he doesn't see everyone, or all ventures as they exist in reality. Instead he pictures them as he wishes. This action can partly be responsible for this period of many disillusionments.

The Public

It's possible that gossip and adverse talk is now flying around in the air. Uncomfortable ordeals may follow.

Nixon may tend to use his emotions to play act so he can gain the sympathy of his audience. However, the curiosity of others can be aroused when he makes unclear statements and omits words.

Pledges may be made that he can't keep. What is uttered one moment can be altered later. It's possible that he doesn't remember what he has said. During this time, Nixon can subconsciously daydream and live in his own wish-fulfilled world.

This nebulous and wishy-washy appearance places him in a bad light. The impression he now makes on the public will most likely be unfavorable. During this time, interviews or broadcasting should be avoided.

* * *

The following is a combination of three progressed aspects. The first aspect (Moon progressed Square MC progressed) starts October 28, 1974. It reaches a peak November 28, 1974 and leaves his chart December 28, 1974.

The second aspect (Moon progressed Parallel MC natal) starts October 1974, It reaches a peak April 24, 1975 and leaves his chart in August 1975.

The third aspect (The MC progressed Opposition the natal Moon) starts April 11, 1975. It reaches a peak April 11, 1976 and leaves his chart April 11, 1977.

By progression the Square and Opposition are discordant; the Parallel is neutral. In his natal chart there is a Trine aspect between the Moon and the MC, therefore, the first and the third aspect are a harmonious and discordant influence and the second aspect can go either way dependent upon how Nixon utilizes it.

NOTE: These aspect have been combined to avoid repetition; also, because the dates overlap.

HOUSES INVOLVED: See page 113 for the Moon's influence. The natal MC is the 10th house cusp. The progressed MC is in the 11th house until February 26, 1976, at which time it will enter the 12th house.

From October 28, 1974 to November 1974, he can attract barriers with work, travel, court and the public. Bad publicity may damage Nixon's image—his reputation can be at stake. Gossip with mixed opinions will probably prevail. Scandal may possibly come through friends or servants.

* * *

This can be a very trying emotional period for Richard Nixon. His moods may fluctuate. Upsets can be attracted. He's probably now adverse to work, however, it's only a momentary whim. He can be away from his desk because of travel, loss of job, or a court appearance. A buddy may possibly save him from difficulties at the last moment.

If he's still President, stormy dissensions with those who work under him may occur. A staff member, or bad publicity can block his efforts toward foreign negotiations. There's a possible strain in Nixon's relationship with the general public, his employees and anyone in another country.

From December 1974 to April 1975, Nixon can experience some fortunate events. He may be lucky in deals involving foreign lands. The public and his aides are likely to be on his side (if he's still President). Good fortune can be attracted through his work. Nixon will probably be given credit for his accomplishments. In return he may glow. Success now can easily be his.

From April 1975 to April 1976, Nixon will attract similar events to the preceding, however, this is a tough emotional period. Lady luck, will most likely pull him through any difficulties which may occur. Many important decisions can now be forced upon him. He may have a problem with concentrating his energies on mental activities. With work, whatever path Nixon chooses to follow, another desired one will possibly be relinquished. Any final big decisions may not be made until April 1976.

* * *

If he's still in public office, something may occur with a subordinate and Nixon has to decide whether he should fire the person, have him resign or try to keep the mess out of the public's eye. Either way, he chooses, there will possibly be trouble with bad publicity or the person speaking in a derogatory manner about Nixon. Gossip can abound, but he will most likely come out on top.

* * *

Perhaps Richard will desire to be with loved ones, but work will possibly dominate the day. Travel can keep him busy and interfere with his home life. Trips may be taken without Patricia. A friend may join him on a jaunt. If this occurs, the reporters will be extremely busy.

* * *

If Nixon is sick, the publicity received about it will possibly cause problems. If progress is now being made with foreign powers, he will not allow any illness to impede his progress. Even though, one side of him may want to quit, another side probably desires to be needed and to help the world through serving his country.

* * *

The following is a combination of three progressed aspects. The first aspect (Moon progressed Trine Sun natal) starts November 17, 1974. It reaches a peak December 17, 1974 and leaves his chart January 17, 1975.

118

The second aspect (Moon progressed Parallel Sun natal) starts in August 1974. It reaches a peak February 20, 1975 and leaves his chart in June 1975.

The third aspect (Moon progressed Sextile Sun progressed) starts February 8, 1975. It reaches a peak March 8, 1975 and leaves his chart April 8, 1975.

By progression, the Trine and Sextile are harmonious; the Parallel is neutral. In his natal chart there is a Semi-sextile aspect between these two planets. A semi-sextile is slightly harmonious; therefore, this is a harmonious influence.

NOTE: These aspects have been combined to avoid repetition; also, because the dates overlap.

HOUSES INVOLVED: See page 113 for the Moon's influence. The Natal Sun is in the 5th house. The Progressed Sun in in the 7th house. The sign Leo is on the 12th house cusp. (The Sun rules Leo.)

Foreign Relationships

Richard Nixon can now possibly be building some solid relationships with foreign powers, the public and his aides or friends (if he's still President, unless he does it for personal gain). The results of his efforts will most likely be more noticeable from November 17 to December 17, 1974, and again from February 8, to March 8, 1975.

Friendly ties can be established. Those who probably will grant him favors consist of the wealthy, influential and powerful class, such as heads of state, royalty, diplomats, politicians and judges. They may wish him well and his position with them can be one of honor.

* * *

International commerce, trade, gold and silver investment is likely to be excellent. Money may flow readily with both the big and little people. The public, in general, may be more favorably inclined toward his various projects. Perhaps Nixon will make an appeal to those matters which will involve their best interests.

* * *

The results of his own labor can now pay off. Nixon may be beaming. His fans will possibly be cheering and applauding. Perhaps some people will begin to have a better opinion of him.

* * *

Nixon will probably treat his subordinates with respect and admiration. He will, most likely, give credit to anyone who deserves it, including anyone in a foreign land.

119

The trips he makes to other countries can bring auspicious publicity. Nixon will probably be favorably received. This is an excellent time for him to broadcast his beliefs and opinions to the world.

* * *

Friends and loved ones may travel with him. If they do, he will likely combine business with pleasure. Because he is proud of his family, he may want to show them to the world. Nixon can have fun on these journeys. The surroundings will probably be regal. Dining may be elegant with the best in silver and gold on the table. Entertainment can be high-class, such as the opera or ballet.

Work

It's possible that Nixon will sometimes work in confined quarters, such as hospitals, while on an airplane, or in a room where he is a guest. Many transactions may occur behind private doors. The negotiations can go well, but will possibly remain secret for a while. The best time for their exposure is November 17 to December 17, 1974 and again February 8 to March 8, 1975.

Court

If he had to appear in court, the judge and jury may now hold him in high esteem. The verdict can be in his favor. Nixon tends to gain, at this time, against all who have opposed him, and he will probably treat his enemies kindly.

Health

The attention he receives from important people, if he is ill, can be impressive. This will possibly satisfy his ego, aid his recovery and increase his vitality and recuperative powers.

* * *

The following aspects starts March 9, 1975. It reaches a peak April 9, and May 20, 1975. The aspect leaves his chart June 20, 1975.

ASPECT: *Moon progressed Sextile Neptune (natal and progressed)*

By progression, this aspect is harmonious. In his natal chart there is no aspect between these two planets; therefore, this is a harmonious influence.

HOUSES INVOLVED: See page 113 for the Moon's influence. The natal Neptune is in the 11th house. The sign Pisces is on the 7th house cusp (Neptune is one of the rulers of Pisces).

Excellent opportunities may be attracted through friends, partners, his help, or foreigners. His idealistic plans may possibly be promoted to the skies. People will probably listen, believe and fall for them. Many promises now made are not likely to be kept. However, this may not faze anyone at this time.

* * *

If Nixon relaxes now by going on a pleasure trip, outing, vacation, or to the theater, he will probably enjoy every moment. His wife or friends may possibly accompany him. Publicity tends to be to his liking. The public could respond favorably and with great interest.

Nixon may dream every night during this time period. He possibly will have prophetic visions. His hunches will probably amaze him; especially when they become a reality. The psychic impressions he now receives should be utilized in his daily contact with others.

* * *

His mate may be placed up on a pedestal now. He may adore Patricia for her humanitarian instincts and the way she behaves with people.

* * *

This is an auspicious time for him to leave the country to promote an oil, gas or petroleum project. However, only 10% of his expectations can be counted on. Nonetheless, he will still be happy with these results.

* * *

If he's still president, immense undertakings with the aviation industry can possibly transpire, or be discussed. Agreements may now be signed with those of other nations. A friend in the aviation field may be involved in an odd way. Publicity may result which links them together. Nixon's reaction most likely will be favorable.

* * *

The following aspect starts October 1974. It reaches a peak April 13 and June 10, 1975. The aspect leaves his chart in October 1975.

ASPECT: *Moon progressed Parallel Jupiter (natal and progressed)*

The next time that these two planets will be in an aspect (listed below) will be on a starting date of November 3, 1975. It reaches a peak December 3, 1975 and leaves his chart January 3, 1976. This same aspect (listed below) will be reactivated again October 10, 1976. It reaches a peak November 10, 1976 and leaves his chart December 10, 1976.

ASPECT: *Moon progressed Inconjunct Jupiter (natal and progressed)*

By progression, the Parallel and the Inconjunct are neutral. In his natal chart there is a Semi-square aspect between these two planets; therefore, this is a slightly discordant influence. *NOTE:* Whenever Jupiter is involved in a neutral aspect it gives a benefic influence; however, the natal discord may add some inharmony to the neutral influence. These aspects have been combined to avoid repetition.

HOUSES INVOLVED: See page 113 for the Moon's influence. The natal and progressed Jupiter are in the 4th house, and the sign Sagittarius is on the 4th house cusp (Jupiter rules Sagittarius). The sign Pisces is on the 7th house cusp (Jupiter is one of the rulers of Pisces).

Foreign Relationships

NOTE: The following paragraphs may apply whether he's President, or not.

Perhaps, the economy of all countries will now gradually be raised. In this direction Nixon tends to be over confident. He may possibly expect trade to be improved to stupendous levels. Importing and exporting can be increased and their prices may be boosted to an all time high. People may aggravate Nixon. Unfavorable comments can be made about his excessive expenditures, trips and unguaranteed business ventures; but he won't care. He's optimistic and in great spirit.

His journeys can cost plenty. The number in his entourage may increase; so can his trips. If anyone suggests a change in the itinerary, it may possibly peeve Nixon. He will probably toss the idea around for a while. If he becomes too indecisive about it he possibly will be quite vexed. However, once he changes his travel plans, he may laugh about his wishy-washiness and thank the person who gave him the suggestion.

* * *

His mood tends to be friendly. The people he encounters can be extremely fond of him. Nixon's happy smile shows everyone how sure he is of all of his transactions. His "share the wealth" philosophy tends to be in.

* * *

It's possible that Nixon can become involved in financial investments abroad with his friends. This may prove fortunate, but Nixon tends to be too hopeful. If the gains are not returned as expected, he will probably appear as if he isn't bothered. And most likely he isn't!

* * *

Those in business, all over the globe, may grant favors to Nixon and his pals. In return, if he's still President, special privileges may be given to them; especially, when they visit the United States.

122

Business

Nixon's calculations can possibly be slightly off-balance. His optimism may be overdone. Annoyances with others can take place, if his financial anticipations are not completely fulfilled. Speedy decisions will have to be avoided; so will his reliance upon others.

* * *

Perhaps the interest rate will be raised. The advice of others, most likely, will not be entirely heeded. The criticism of others can make Nixon indecisive, at this time. He can swing from a mood of being happy-go-lucky to one of irritation.

* * *

His friends may encourage him to expand in real estate. Nixon's holdings can slowly increase. If he wishes to sell property now, he may not receive the enormous sum he desires. However, it's probable that a profit will be made.

The Public

He can attract an increase of publicity, at this time. Most of it may be favorable. Nixon will probably become peeved, if anyone throws a sarcasm his way. Perhaps, he'll act as if he doesn't care.

* * *

When surrounded by the public, he may beam and shake their hands; they'll probably smile back. Nixon can reassure and inspire others. Statements can be made that are beyond the truth. Most likely the working class will believe some of his exaggerated promises.

* * *

Perhaps, increases will be given to his employees. This may appear in the form of money, a favor or an expensive gift. His mood is likely to be one of great generosity. If he's still President, members of his staff may travel with him. He can and will, probably, treat them all as a close friend.

Court

Lawsuits can annoy him, however, his assurance can cover up any minor apprehensions. If he does well in court now, he may brag about it. His words will probably be shifted and exaggerated.

Home

He may take Patricia and his home for granted. While Nixon is in his abode, he can tend to be cheerful. Pat may encourage him. There's a tendency for him to be in a giving and sharing mood with her. Happiness is with his wife; therefore, he may want to be with her most of the time. To do so, travel will be necessary on her part.

Health

Nixon tends to gain weight now from over-eating. He should guard against indulging in rich, fatty and spicy foods. But he probably won't care.

* * *

Growths or tumors can be attracted, while under this aspect.

* * *

The following aspect starts in December 1974. It reaches a peak June 15, 1975 and leaves his chart in October 1975.

ASPECT: Moon progressed Parallel Mercury (natal)

When the Parallel aspect is in there will also be a shorter period when another type aspect will be made. The starting date of the latter will be May 4, 1975. It reaches a peak June 4, 1975 and leaves his chart July 4, 1975.

ASPECT: Moon progressed Semi-square Mercury progressed

The next time that these two planets are in aspect to each other will be on a starting date of September 17, 1975. A peak is reached October 17, 1975 and leaves November 17, 1975.

ASPECT: Moon progressed Inconjunct Mercury (natal)

By progression, the Parallel and Inconjunct are neutral; the Semi-square is discordant. In his natal chart there is no aspect between these two planets; therefore, the influence will be neutral while the neutral aspect is in and discordant while the Semi-square aspect is in. Under the neutral aspect the influence can be harmonious and discordant, dependent upon how Nixon utilizes it.

NOTE: These aspects have been combined to avoid repetition; also, because the dates overlap.

HOUSES INVOLVED: See page 113 for the Moon's influence. The sign Virgo is on the first house cusp (Mercury rules Virgo.) The natal Mercury is in the 4th house. The progressed Mercury is in the 7th house. The sign Gemini is on the 10th house cusp (Mercury rules Gemini.)

Foreign Relationships

If Nixon's still in office, the following may occur: Nixon's mental activities can increase to greater intensity regarding documents, papers, contracts, agreements or treaties. His mind tends to fluctuate now; therefore, he may be indecisive during this period about signing anything important. A problem may have to be solved before Nixon places his signature on any dotted line.

124

His wishy-washy attitude can make him become irritated with himself; especially, when he has to make a decision which involves a change. The worst period, where confusion is a daily occurrence, is from May 4, 1975, to June 4, 1975. From September 17, 1975 to November 17, 1975, he probably will not be as peeved or mentally disturbed. Whatever his thoughts or resolutions are, at this time, nothing much comes of them.

* * *

Misunderstandings can occur and communications can be off with employees, women, the wife, the public (in every land), or with those in power overseas. Nixon's true intentions may not come across. It's also possible that his translator may not interpret what is being said in the proper perspective. Minor annoyances will probably be felt by everyone.

* * *

A staff member, if Nixon's still President, may misconstrue something which causes utter chaos. If he's not in office, it can be an employee that creates the same problem. Perhaps, Nixon will make unwise changes with those who work for him, or he may switch their chores around. It's possible that his life is turned upside-down now. If this is the case, it may explain why he probably acts uncertain, apprehensive and indecisive.

* * *

The following are a few examples of his high strung tendencies which are now being activated:
An employee or partner of his may be unpunctual with a phone call. If this occurs. Nixon will probably fidget and pace the floor.
Perhaps, Richard is on a trip and suddenly receives news which needs a quick solution. Nervousness and a possible change of plans may result.

* * *

Because of problems with his partner or staff (if he's still in office), his personal affairs may be altered. He tends to be uneasy and restless. Nixon may desire to spend time with his family, but will probably have to adjust to quick changes which can possibly take him away from those he loves.
NOTE: The preceding section applies whether he is, or is not, President.

Publicity
His worst period for the following (under this section) is from May 4, 1975 to June 4, 1975.

He may not speak clearly while appearing before the public, or with the press. Nixon is likely to be misquoted, or the populace and reporters can criticize him quite strongly. People may not approve of his words or actions. The disapproval tends to be chiefly toward his travels, transcripts or the signing of agreements.

* * *

His itinerary is subject to change daily. Nixon, and everyone else connected with his travels, may be indecisive about what countries should be visited. Once a place is chosen, the journey may be altered. A phone call, correspondence or bad publicity may be responsible for the new plans that have to be made.

Work

Nixon can now be mentally and emotionally upset. This tends to be a moody and restless period for him. This may be due to his mind being clogged with too many preoccupations regarding foreign deals, trips and personal matters. He's in a period when he can become easily bored because he needs variety with work and deviations from his daily personal routine. Attracted could be confusion with the telephone, people and distractions which make it difficult for him to concentrate.

* * *

A stoppage in mid-course, and not completing that which has been started, must be guarded against. Possibly, involved is everyday chores, trips or the signing of documents. It's not a favorable time to write his name on any important paper.

* * *

Nixon must be careful, at this time, of any unwise and impulsive changes, especially with new laws, bills or any matter which will require his signature on the dotted line.

Those Who Work Under Him

The following (under this section) is most likely to occur from May 4, 1975 to June 4, 1975.

Transcripts, or important papers, may have omissions, inaccuracies or mistakes. His extreme criticism may bring attention to his displeasure with others. What probably really bothers him is that he neglects to catch the errors that they make.

Nixon may receive unreliable messages from his subordinates. Because of them, difficulties can be attracted which can possibly make him switch his views or plans.

Newspaper and magazine coverage can increase. Many books written about Nixon may now be published. Possibly, a transcript can be the talk of the day. A paper shortage is likely to create pandemonium. At this time, the following may ensue: Gossip, scandal, confusion, difficulties with the public or those who work under him.

If an important decision has to be made, Nixon should avoid doing so from May 4, 1975 to June 4, 1975, as he may make the wrong one. He should be calm, patient and keep silent. If he doesn't, the public will probably go against him now.

If he discusses any problem with a friend, wife, lawyers, or subordinate, each will probably have a different solution. This will probably increase his indecisiveness to the point of utter confusion.

Personal Concerns

Many distractions, restlessness and personal changes can occur. Gossip may be in about his private life or his health. Communication may be a problem which can result in misunderstandings. Partnerships or real estate deals can constantly alter, or Nixon may deviate from his plans regarding these areas.

His health can fluctuate. It's chiefly his nerves, circulation or stomach. Emotions may run high and create some of the difficulty. He will have to control these areas, especially, from May 4 to June 4, 1975.

From September 17 to November 17, 1975, his moods can fluctuate more than ever before, such as the following instance: He may one moment desire to

127

take a trip; the next, he doesn't. An idea to sign, or talk over, a new agreement can possibly occur; however, nothing much will probably come of it. A press conference may be desired, but Nixon decides he doesn't feel like talking. He may expect foreign trade to expand, but it doesn't. To invest in real estate or business in another country may sound good to him, but nothing results of his idea. To make a change with property, or his house may be thought about, but unless he pushes it into action, it will probably be null and void.

Nixon may desire to tell Patricia a newsworthy item, but may decide against it. It's possible that he may think that if he tells her his future plans, they may be altered and she would be disappointed. A changeableness, on his part, can create some minor disturbance in the home.

* * *

The following aspect starts July 6, 1975. It reaches a peak from August 6 to September 16, 1975, and leaves his chart October 16, 1975.

ASPECT: Moon progressed in a Conjunction to Saturn (natal and progressed).

By progression, this is a highly discordant aspect. In his natal chart, there is a Square and a Parallel aspect between these two planets; therefore, this is a discordant influence.

HOUSES INVOLVED: See page 113 for the Moon's influence. The sign Capricorn is on the 5th house cusp. (Saturn rules Capricorn.) The sign Aquarius is on the 6th house cusp. (Saturn is one of the rulers of Aquarius.) The natal and progressed Saturn are in the 9th house.

Foreign Relationships

Delays, postponements and hindrances can be attracted with trips, importing and exporting, important negotiations, stock investments on the foreign market, or the entertainment of people from abroad.

Everything may appear to be at a temporary standstill. There can possibly be a shortage of supplies. Nixon may have red tape or restrictions, with customs because of the rules and regulations which are enforced.

During this time, Nixon can be extremely shrewd, clever and selfish to gain his desired ends. He may use people in any bargains or transactions.

Work

A tendency now to do deep, practical, logical and careful thinking. His subconscious mind may be busy calculating, so everything will resolve in his favor. Nixon will possibly use strategy and plan all moves with preciseness.

* * *

He can patiently wait for his gains, although a part of him is restless, bored and desires a change. His negativity will probably be noticed by everyone who

128

is in daily contact with him. Depressed and worried, he may feel weighed down with heavy burdens. Shortages of food or goods may be a bigger problem than admitted. A general lack of the everyday necessities may mean extra work so he can solve the problems.

* * *

Nixon can be greatly concerned about the public; however, he may not *feel* like talking about a slump, recession, depression or any distress areas. However, silence may reign; or possibly, he may delay a lecture. If he does give a speech it probably will be serious, with many things left unsaid.

* * *

If he's still President, the populace may dislike Nixon if he places a freeze on wages, or a limit on food and other supplies. He may feel it is his responsibility to use foresight now regarding raw materials, importing and exporting. Nixon may clamp down on small business people, roll back prices and create fear in the general public. Regardless of his position, he may feel helpless that he is unable to aid those who are in need.

* * *

Perhaps, he will outline a plot which others, including foreign powers, will reject. A few of their proposals Nixon may turn down. Whichever way he moves, there will probably be someone who will try to block his efforts.

* * *

Any bitterness felt toward the ex-members of his staff will most likely be kept within. He possibly may want self-imposed privacy and to avoid contacts with others. His suspicion of people, or deals, can prove correct.

Court
If a court case is pending it may be delayed. The outcome will probably be a big worry of his. Nixon may fear a loss and, at this time, it is possible. If he appeared before a judge or jury, he most likely will use extreme caution with every word spoken. Perhaps, an ex-aide or friend, will testify against him.

Stock Market
Nixon tends to be overly cautious now. He's not in the mood to gamble or take unnecessary risks. If a friend gives him advice, he may not act upon it. At this time he probably doesn't trust anyone. If he buys stock now, it may prove

worthless. Nixon can possibly become emotionally panic-stricken if the stock market starts to plunge downward, especially if any losses occur.

The Public

Publicity can be bad. If there are shortages, Nixon may limit everyone to only one of each item (if he's still President). This can create much dislike among the people. They will probably react unfavorably to all of his actions, at this time.

Personal Concerns

Food may be hoarded in his household. His servants may possibly steal from him. Nixon may be suspicious of thievery; therefore, he may have everything under lock and key.

* * *

Domestic problems can bug him such as: He can be worried about the health of someone (of the female sex) close to him; family upsets may occur; his children can be a chief source of difficulty; the safety and welfare of his loved ones is important to him; therefore, he may now make plans for their future; he's not likely to participate in any pleasurable activity now; he may feel indifferent towards sex.

Health

He's probably emotionally exhausted due to his negative thinking. Health problems may cause him to worry. Constipation can be a problem. His circulation may be poor. Constriction in the veins and "charley horses" are likely. He can be susceptible to colds.

His system may lack calcium, and minerals because he isn't assimilating them properly. Variety is needed in his diet. He may not have an appetite now. Boredom may exist if he's eating bland foods. However, Nixon can discipline himself to sticking with his regimen.

* * *

The following aspect has always been in Nixon's chart (Pluto progressed Parallel natal Moon), but will be reinforced starting July 21, 1975. It reaches a peak August 21 and September 8, 1975. This reinforced aspect (listed below) will leave his chart October 8, 1975. The reinforced aspect is a Semi-sextile which is different than the Parallel that has always been in his chart. *NOTE:* These aspects have been combined to avoid repetition; also, because the dates overlap.

ASPECT: *Moon progressed Semi-sextile Pluto (natal and progressed)*

By progression, the Parallel is neutral; the Semi-sextile, is slightly harmonius. In his natal chart, there is a Trine aspect between these two planets; therefore, this is a harmonious influence. Whenever Nixon uses the traits and actions of these two planets, luck will most likely follow.

HOUSES INVOLVED: See page 113 for the Moon's influence. The sign Scorpio is on the 3rd house cusp. (Pluto is one of the rulers of Scorpio.) The natal and progressed Pluto are in the 10th house.

Work

His hunches in business or with subordinates should be heeded. If a compulsive desire to take action in a specific direction is felt, he should follow it.

From July 21, 1975 to October 21, 1975, Nixon may swear that he KNOWS he must attend to certain matters, regardless of how others try to sway him.

* * *

This can be a busy time for him with many consultations. His office may be as crowded as Grand Central Station. He can have unusual sources of information. Any investigation Nixon had performed on another can now prove to his benefit. Special reports may be tucked away for future use.

* * *

It's possible that a political party will make a business agreement with Nixon. It may involve a backing of a candidate. Perhaps, some form of a mutual exchange takes place between Nixon and the person running for office. All offers, at this time, can be rewarding for Nixon.

* * *

He can possibly be involved in joint operations in business. Corporations may appeal to him. World-wide deals tend to be favorable. Granting privileges to others will probably benefit him.

* * *

To take part in meetings and support the claims of others may keep Nixon active. Most likely he will have an objective in mind, which can possibly reward everyone concerned.

131

* * *

If he's still in power and there are strikes, Nixon may intervene. He might feel it's part of his duty in helping the country. Others can be manipulated to do his bidding.

It's possible that he will make demands upon the public to cooperate with his compulsory rules. After all, he most likely believes that they are for the betterment of all concerned. Lady Luck is riding right along with him now. The majority of the people will probably go along with his desires.

The Public

This is a favorable time for Nixon to give a special report by the television media, *if* the following is involved: Humanitarian endeavors, world peace or business that will aid everyone and bring world-wide prosperity.

Foreign Relationships

He should follow his first impressions whenever he deals with people overseas.

* * *

Many trips abroad are possibly in the offering. The crowds will probably be friendly. Tours of plants can prove beneficial. Joint space programs may be launched (if he's still President). The representatives of the nations involved will probably meet for the ceremonies.

* * *

Corporations, franchises, mergers and chain operations may be organized with various countries participating in these ventures. Everything planned may be on a universal basis. Assembly line production which utilizes the latest discoveries of each nation may be part of the deal.

Commissions, leagues and investigating committees can be established. Everyone will probably have a strong cooperative spirit in this joint project. A pleasant atmosphere is likely to prevail.

* * *

International court could possibly be held and the new laws may be agreed upon, or placed into effect (if he's still President). These changes can involve importing and exporting, missiles, or atomic plants.

* * *

If Nixon uses a go-between for any foreign deals, the results will probably prove fortunate. Formal treaties, or agreements, may be signed which can possibly bring luck to everyone concerned (if he's still President).

* * *

Mass production of supplies may be shipped, but because of another aspect in Nixon's chart, a delay or some obstacle can occur. The problem may be a shortage, or deal with some of Nixon's subordinates. Most likely the public will react to this with mixed feelings (if he's still President).

Work
While traveling. Nixon's intellectual activity can be increased. Reading will probably be compulsive. Reports may be studied and quick action will possibly be taken.

* * *

Telephone calls from his representatives (if he's still in power) can be more numerous now than at any other time. With these conversations, Nixon will most likely go along with the idea of his intermediary; however, there may be some revisions or amendments to contracts or the constitution.

* * *

NOTE: If he's still President, or while in office, the following applies:
Many members of his staff will probably cooperate with his efforts toward peace, mass production, nuclear power plants, missile bases, or outer space programs. Also, some special labor union deals with industry may please everyone concerned. If action is taken, along with any of these lines, fortunate results are likely to be obtained.

Court
If Nixon has to appear in court he should cooperate with investigating committees because something favorable is likely to happen. Groups or friends may possibly band together in his behalf. Past efforts for world-peace and foreign negotiations might aid his case.

NOTE: The preceeding applies if there are no discordant Moon progressions up to January 1977.

* * *

133

The following aspect starts February 1975. It reaches a peak August 24, 1975 and leaves his chart December 24, 1975.

ASPECT: *Moon progressed Parallel Mars natal*

These two planets will be in another type aspect (listed below) starting September 10, 1975. A peak is reached October 10, 1975 and leaves his chart November 10, 1975.

ASPECT: *Moon progressed Inconjunct Mars natal*

By progression, the Parallel and Inconjunct are neutral; however, because Mars is involved discord is added. In his natal chart there are no aspects between these two planets; therefore, this is a slightly discordant influence.

NOTE: These aspects have been combined to avoid repetition; also, because the dates overlap.

HOUSES INVOLVED: See page 113 for the Moon's influence. The sign Scorpio is on the 3rd house cusp. (Mars is one of the rulers of Scorpio.) The natal Mars is in the 4th house. The progressed Mars is in the 5th house. The sign Aries is on the 8th house cusp. (Mars rules Aries.)

Home

Tensions can build quite heavily as August 4, 1975 approaches. It's possible that an automobile will have mechanical problems, which can anger Nixon. He may take it out on those near and dear to him. At this time, he tends to be irritable and quarrelsome; especially, with family, friends or employees.

Domestic problems won't amount to much from September 10 to November 10, 1975. He will possibly desire to tell someone off, but may refrain from speaking. If he loses his temper, people will probably *not* pay it any heed.

* * *

His sexual drive can become stronger as August 4, 1975 approaches. Problems may occur with women, or sex. Strife can be with love-making, or about it. For instance: It's possible that he's in a hurry with the bedroom scene.

Work

He can initiate things and get the ball rolling. With some of his help he may be short and brusque over the phone. Employees may possibly labor overtime. Nixon will probably expect the work to be completed "right now."

His staff, if he's still President, may resent him. Jealousy abounds; so does competition. Perhaps, Nixon will fight back. He most likely will try everything to win, in spite of any opposition.

134

A few cuss words may be bandied about, as the working environment becomes hot and heavy. If employees disagree with him, Nixon's temper will probably be shown. It's possible that he'll want to get rid of an aide (if he's still in office). The person can be sent off at a distance, or on a tour which will involve extensive traveling.

* * *

NOTE: The following may apply whether he's President or not; the problems attracted can be with an aide, or anyone working for him.

Complications in transactions may occur with his representatives. He can possibly feel impatient for quick results, but his go-between may move too slow. Nixon has to now take care that he doesn't leap into any bad situations. His aimless changes can attract uncomfortable trials and tribulations. Nixon's desires may be ungratified. Staff members or the help will probably gossip. If the rumors return to his ears, he may be furious.

Foreign Relationships
Quick trips may be taken by Nixon. Antagonism from others can occur because of his jumping into deals which involve other countries.

* * *

If he's still President, Nixon will have to exercise extreme caution that he doesn't try to help a war torn country by sending troops there, or giving financial aid. If he does, the public will probably have their own battle going against him.

* * *

His main downfall, now, can be his subconscious mind reacting too fast with important decisions. The action taken, most likely, has not been thought-out in it's proper perspective.

The Public
Nixon may feel tense; especially, if he's put on the spot. If he speaks to the populace he has to watch his remarks. He tends to be hasty and may say everything right to the point. A lack of diplomacy now can create problems and bad publicity such as public quarrels or people overseas turning against him.

If his family is in hot water with financial problems, the news will be known to one and all. Nixon may talk about his debts, taxes, loans or friends. His real estate operations, especially, with his brothers, can be out in the open. This in a sense may anger Nixon.

Money

His tax problems can build to a worse state than they were previously in. Loans from friends may be granted to help pay them off. His debts can continue to pile to larger sums. It may be necessary for Nixon to borrow more money. The obligations he has tends to bother him and he may take it out on those close to him.

* * *

The taxpayer's money may be spent haphazardly (if he's still President). If so, outrages with the public will probably result. Nixon can now attract antagoism quite easily. His friends and loved ones may disagree with his spending sprees or trips.

* * *

He may be angry if he plunges into stock market transactions and doesn't fair well. His gambling spirit is strong, but it can cost him plenty.

Court

He has to be careful of cracking under stress and strain regarding any court matter or procedure. His temper is likely to be shown at the drop of a hat. If Nixon now speaks up too harshly, or hastily, he will probably be in a real predicament.

Health

Accidents can happen, or some one may take a shot at him. These events can occur while he's in a car, or at home. If he's walking too fast, his ankle may not support him properly, which can result in a fall.

* * *

Operations may be necessary. Fever, cuts, sores, burns and rashes can be attracted.

* * *

NOTE: The following is not an aspect, but a change of Nixon's progressed Moon from one sign to another.

Since June 1973, Nixon's progressed Moon has been in the sign Taurus (the bull). The Moon will remain here until October 7, 1975. On this date it will enter into the sign Gemini, until January 1978.

The Moon in Taurus tends to make him stubborn, plodding and practical. He can take an interest in material possessions. Emotionally Nixon can endure plenty (like the bull), until the right moment arrives to let go.

* * *

When the Moon leaves Taurus to enter Gemini, everyone will notice that his set ways (Taurus) have changed into adaptable ones (Gemini).

The Moon in Gemini will allow his subconscious mind to make quick adjustments. He will probably be emotionally and mentally changeable at the same time (a real Jekyll and Hyde). His emotions may flit in various directions. Curiosity and restlessness can reign.

* * *

The following aspect starts December 23, 1975. It reaches a peak January 23, 1976 and leaves his chart February 23, 1976.

ASPECT: *Moon progressed Square Venus natal*

By progression, this is a discordant aspect. In his natal chart, there is no aspect between these two planets; therefore, this is a discordant influence.

HOUSES INVOLVED: See page 113 for the Moon's influence. The sign Libra is on the 2nd house cusp (Venus rules Libra). The natal Venus is in the 6th house. The progressed Venus is in the 8th house. The sign Taurus is on the 9th house cusp (Venus rules Taurus).

Foreign Relationships

Nixon's desire to travel overseas may be blocked by problems with his health, work or money. If he does take a long distance trip, he may not feel up to it. However, he will probably give in to the easy way out and go.

NOTE: This is not a favorable time for him to journey abroad. He may not make a good impression upon the public. The praise and adulation he craves will not be given to him now. It's probable that the working class is against him because of duties or taxes he might have placed upon their goods which are imported to the U.S.A., or possibly because of scandal, bad publicity, or the position he now holds (jobwise).

Difficulties can be attracted whenever Nixon gives expensive gifts, with the taxpayer's money, to people overseas (if he's still the President). The public may cry out that the present is not worth the price paid, or that their money should be spent for worthwhile projects. While in public office, if he receives a gift from someone in another country, Nixon will probably be upset because he will not be able to claim it as his *OWN* personal possession.

* * *

He may be in an anti-social mood. Perhaps, it's because he isn't feeling well. However, if a social affair involves important business, he will probably accept the invitation. At the gathering, his charm will be turned on, and no one will know that he's possibly bored.

It's probable that people can easily influence him now, because he's in the mood to please others. Approval from them, at this time, might be necessary. Nixon will probably do almost anything to gain peace.

Money

Whether he's President, or not, the devaluation of the dollar may create hindrances when Nixon deals with various countries. Currancy problems can bring dissensions. Whichever way Nixon turns, he may possibly have the public, here and abroad, against him.

* * *

He's now likely to be in a spending mood, which means, he can go on a spree with *his* money. It may be spent on clothes, jewelry, art, gifts, or on tips to waiters and servants. His tipping can be overdone. If he gives a present to someone and the person doesn't appear delighted, Nixon's feelings will probably be hurt.

* * *

If he's still President, it's possible that the taxpayer's money will now be used thoughtlessly. Luxury items can be purchased. The price paid for food, entertainment and trips will probably be out of line. The public will most likely be against him. If he spends other peoples currency on expensive jewelry, this probably will create an uproar.

Problems may result with his loved ones, staff (if he's still President) or the general populace. Possibly, no one will approve of his heavy expenditures. Nixon may have to borrow money from a pal to make a payment on his taxes or a loan. Any personal debts he has can now receive bad publicity.

Work

Obstacles can be in the way with those who work for him. They may not agree with his actions or beliefs. Nixon may try to be nice to them; however, if they don't respond favorably his sensitivity may show.

His staff, if he's still in power, can now walk over him. He's likely to be in a submissive mood. At this time, Nixon can be changeable, uncertain, bored, and may crave variety. He should finish that which he starts. Any aimless and unwise decisions Nixon makes has to be guarded against.

At this time a possible lazy streak can be felt. To relax and rest by taking a vacation could be what's preying on his subconscious mind. But it won't do him much good because there probably will be interferences with these pursuits.

If he expresses his beliefs and opinions outwardly, barriers can be created. Especially. if a friend, loved one or aide (if he's still President) doesn't agree with him. An emotional reaction may set in, but they'll never know it.

Court
To avoid lawsuits, or court action, Nixon can pay plenty. If he had to appear in court, he probably would be completely shattered if a friend or an ex-staff member testified against him.

Loved Ones
It's possible that Nixon is frustrated with love and affections. The obstacle may be the result of problems with health, work, money or trips. At this time, the least little thing that a cherished one says is likely to hurt his feelings. However, he tends to keep everything within.

Health
Trouble can occur with the veins, skin, or hair. The phlebitis may create difficulty with work, travel and in social areas. If Nixon is in pain, no one will know it.

Food may be served, at social functions that he doesn't like, or that is against his diet. Most likely, he will give in and eat it. Later, it may disagree with him. Sweets and starches, at this time, may not assimilate properly in his system.

* * *

The following aspect starts January 18, 1976. It reaches a peak February 18, 1976 and leaves his chart March 18, 1976.

ASPECT: *Moon progressed Sesqui-square Sun natal*

By progression, this is a discordant aspect. In his natal chart there is a Semi-sextile aspect between these two planets; which is slightly harmonious. The progressed aspects discord will over-balance the natal harmony; therefore, this is a discordant influence.

HOUSES INVOLVED: See page 113 for the Moon's influence. The natal Sun is in the 5th house. The progressed Sun is in the 7th house. The sign Leo is on the 12th house cusp. (The Sun rules Leo.)

Work

Nixon can be bored and restless. Variety may be desired. The applause for a job well done may *not* be received. He may forge ahead, only to be knocked down. The upsets that take place can be shattering to his vanity.

One after another aggravation may be had with his job, employees, enemies, staff (if he's still in power). The episodes which transpire can affect his ego. Most likely he won't feel important. His pride may be damaged. Emotional reactions can set in. Nixon will probably stew and wonder if there is a better way of handling everything.

* * *

This is a period when his plans can go asunder. Jolts may occur. Friends and staff members (if he's still President) can catch him off guard. Perhaps his efforts to gain recognition are blocked. Unexpected changes seem to abound.

* * *

A person working under him may receive the credit for a foreign transaction which originally was Nixon's idea. It's possible that Richard will be blamed for things he didn't do. The general populace may not favor him now. Publicity will probably not be to his liking. His self esteem and power can be lessened.

Nixon's liable to be in a bossy mood. Perhaps, within himself, he feels inferior; therefore, he compensates by dominating others. People can now hold him back from accomplishing his aims. This can agitate him.

His next move will probably be to control everyone through making rules. Most likely he will make sure that his authority is noticed. However, when others don't react *his* way, it will create a mental and physical upheaval within himself.

140

* * *

Perhaps speeches made to the public will not go over now. If he is backing a candidate, his ego can be hurt through the person.

* * *

It's possible that his rivals will tear him apart publicly. It may surprise Nixon if a friend, who is also an aide (present or former), now becomes his competitor and enemy.

Foreign Relationships

NOTE: The following can apply in any type of occupation—as President or a businessman. Current and prevailing situations may take Nixon away from his job. His destination can be overseas. There's a possibility that disturbances with foreign nations can bring many changes. Nixon may now have a few doors close but others can open.

* * *

Nixon is likely to be upset with the public, his staff (if he's still in public office), or someone in a foreign nation. The common class may not agree with him. He can have trouble with men of power, rank, wealth, influence, or anyone in an authoritative position. His egotistical demeanor can possibly alienate everyone. Nixon will, perhaps, be emotionally hurt by the way others behave towards him.

He will probably try to figure how he can have his own way and make the necessary changes that others are demanding. At this time, his stubbornness and ego are likely to be his downfall.

Court

His nose may be up in the air if he has to appear in front of a judge or jury. However, he will be dignified. There's a tendency for him to feel that he is above others and beyond reproach.

If he has a lawsuit, it will possibly interfere with his business, pleasure and power. People may think less of him now. His travel plans can be changed because of legal matters.

Investments

Fluctuations may be easily attracted now if he has invested in the stock market. Nixon should avoid the foreign exchange at this time. Inside tips by friends or important people may create a few upheavals; especially, when the forecasts don't come true.

Friends

Secret business deals can possibly take place with his pals. These affairs can involve foreign transactions, or people in powerful positions. Perhaps, Nixon will not want to draw any attention to these matters; however, they may be discovered and brought to light.

If his hush-hush activities are now publicly acknowledged, commotion and excitement will reign. Nixon will be let down if a buddy is to blame for their exposure.

* * *

Nixon and a pal may plan a trip. If the person cancels with him, his ego will probably be hurt. Or, it's possible that they will travel together and this action brings bad publicity. Perhaps, the press will think that the two of them are in a business partnership which involves international trade, and Nixon is using political excuses (if he's still President) for his overseas journey.

Loved ones

Agitations may occur if his daughter files for a divorce, or perhaps, his son-in-law does something to upset him. Nixon's domestic problems can receive slightly discordant publicity; this will probably disturb him.

* * *

Nixon may be in a mood to show Patricia off now. His pride can be hurt if she doesn't travel with him, or make a public appearance. It's possible that Pat will make excuses which hurt his feelings. In turn, to save face, he may alibi for her.

* * *

Work and travel can interfere with his pleasures. Love making can be a hassle. Sex may possibly shake his ego.

Health

His constitution and vitality can be lessened now. Nixon's stamina may be impaired. People seem to drain him of his usual pep and energy. Perhaps, any liveliness he feels is the result of sheer subbornness to press forward.

An emotional exhaustion may take place, if he brags or his efforts to gain self-esteem are thwarted. He will probably attract people who will constantly try to knock his ego down.

* * *

The following aspect started March 11, 1974. It reaches a peak in early January 1977 and leaves his chart April 17, 1980.

ASPECT: *Venus progressed Parallel Moon natal*

These two planets will be in another type aspect (listed below) starting February 18, 1976. A peak is reached March 18, 1976 and leaves his chart April 18, 1976.

ASPECT: *Moon progressed Semi-sextile Venus progressed*

By progression, the Parallel is neutral; the Semi-sextile, is slightly harmonious. In his natal chart, there is no aspect between these two planets; therefore, the influence will be harmonious.

NOTE: These aspects have been combined to avoid repetition also, because these dates overlap.

HOUSES INVOLVED: See page 113 for the Moon's influence. The sign Libra is on the 2nd house cusp. (Venus rules Libra.) The natal Venus is in the 6th house. The progressed Venus is in the 8th house. The sign Taurus is on the 9th house cusp. (Venus rules Taurus.)

Social life

There can be a gradual increase of more receptions, banquets and entertainments (abroad and in the U.S.A.) as January 1977 approaches.

He can cultivate wise affiliations with those overseas. Favorable opportunities may be presented if he entertains anyone from society.

* * *

During this time, Nixon can become somewhat lazy. A mood to have fun may be more noticeable as January 1977 arrives. His interest can be to relax and enjoy his travels, friends and loved ones. Greater intensity may be felt, in this direction, as January 1977 is approached.

* * *

From February 18, 1976 to March 18, 1976, he can have a pleasant time in foreign countries. The gatherings will most likely be elegant. Nixon can be well received. His business may be enhanced through social contact.

Personality

Nixon can gain from being cheerful and nice to those who work under him, loved ones, friends, the public, and a judge or jury.

Gifts and Money

As January 1977 approaches, many expensive presents can be given and received from various countries. These items may be costly. Jewelry and art could be part of the exchange. Most likely gifts may arrive which Nixon will graciously accept. They could be from employees or loved ones.

If he is ill, beautiful get-well cards may be sent to him by the public. The thoughtfulness of others will probably please him.

* * *

Amusements, fun and trips can cost plenty. The amount spent is likely to increase more as January 1977 approaches. The sums disbursed may be the taxpayer's (if he's still President) or his own. He might have to pay gift tax on certain items.

* * *

The value of the dollar can slowly rise. It's possible that there is a gradual flow of more currency being exchanged between the United States and other countries. If Nixon's still in power, he may encourage people to travel and spend their money more freely.

* * *

Nixon can receive publicity about his generosity to maids, servants, attendants, waiters, loved ones and friends. His big tipping days don't end now, they seem to increase.

* * *

He can earn money easily now. His mood may be to keep it in circulation. Cash will probably leave his bank account as fast as it comes in. Attention will be paid to his bills, loans and taxes. Nixon would not want these areas overlooked.

Loved Ones
Subconsciously, he will probably love those close to him more with each passing day. His beautiful feelings of affection can be intensified as January 1977 approaches.

* * *

The following aspect starts December 1, 1975. It reaches a peak January 1, 1976 and leaves his chart February 1, 1976. The aspect will commence again March 8, 1976. It reaches a peak April 8, 1976 and leaves his chart May 8, 1976.

ASPECT: *Moon progressed Trine Uranus (natal and progressed)*

By progression, this is a harmonious aspect. In his natal chart, there is no aspect between these two planets; therefore, this is a harmonious influence.

HOUSES INVOLVED: See page 113 for the Moon's influence. The natal and progressed Uranus are in the 5th house. The sign Aquarius is on the 6th house cusp. (Uranus is one of the rulers of Aquarius.)

Work
If he's still President, Nixon is likely to make sudden changes in the government, with his staff, or adopt new policies with foreign nations. Good luck and unusual conditions can result. He can attract fortunate business transactions now. His plans may possibly alter. However, any adjustments he needs to make can easily be made. At this time, Lady Luck is likely to appear through other people—friends, loved ones, foreigners, employees or his staff (if he's still in public office). A new job will possibly be offered to him.

* * *

Those who work under him may surprise him with a new and unusual idea, invention, or approach to business. Electricity or electronics can, in some way, be involved. These unheard of and untried projects can prove fortunate for Nixon.

* * *

His mind may be on a high mental level. Ideas can pop into his thoughts from out of left field. His intuition may be strong; he should follow it.

* * *

This can be a favorable time, for Nixon, to make changes with his staff, employees, or to talk to the public (if he's still in power).

* * *

Nixon's mind can be blown sky-high whenever he talks to someone and knows what the person is thinking, and how the individual will react to his suggestions.

New laws may be passed in the court regarding taxes, pensions, social security or unemployment insurance. Whatever is approved at this time can be beneficial for everyone.

NOTE: Action of this type can affect Nixon regardless of the position he holds—President, or otherwise.

Foreign Countries
This can be an auspicious time for him to take a sudden and spur-of-the-moment trip. It may result in good luck with people in other lands. From out

145

of the clear blue sky, new deals and conditions can be attracted. Agreements may be signed quickly. The relationship between the United States and these other nations can prove to be extremely fortunate (if he's still the President).

* * *

Entertaining can be unusual. The performers in a show may fascinate Nixon. The interesting manner in which he is amused can be an unforgettable experience. New alliances and friendships may result.

The Public
Whenever Nixon expresses his beliefs and opinions outwardly, good fortune may come smiling his way. He knows what to say for the best given effect. And it works! In fact, he can now mesmerize his audience.

The general populace can be so hypnotized by his words and action that there is a favorable change in public opinion about him. People will probably go right along with whatever he says.

* * *

All of his ordeals can prove fortunate. Sudden television shows may be in Nixon's favor. He should take advantage of every possible moment. The public can be in the palm of his hand.

* * *

If he had to appear in court, an unusual ruling, verdict or decree can occur. Nixon has a great chance now of winning any case. He may be saved at the last minute by someone he least expects. Those who might possibly come to his aid now include his loved ones, friends, acquaintances, employees, staff members (if he's still in power), ex-aides, or someone from another country.

* * *

Stock Market
The foreign exchange can be lucky. Favored is electronics; computers; wiring or electrical items; gadgets; inventions; automobiles; or stock in a company which has new plants (power or electrical), new equipment or products.

Personal Life
Loved ones can bring pleasant surprises, fun and good fortune with publicity, business, travel, foreigners and new ideas.

146

Nixon may feel free and independent now. Pleasures can be had with sports and games. He is likely to take up a new hobby. It may not last but it can hold his attention for a while.

* * *

His mind is receptive to anything that is out of the ordinary. A new philosophy or religion can be studied. The occult world may fascinate him. Astrology or metaphysics can absorb his time.

He can attract these areas through the female sex and his family, friends or employees. It may make him feel that his whole life now has a different meaning. New conditions can open as a result of the change he makes within himself.

* * *

Nixon may attract a new love into his life. It can be in the form of a woman, or a pastime diversion. If he meets someone while on a trip in another country, or at a party, he can possibly be spellbound.

They may have a sudden love affair, or a platonic relationship. The person can continue to keep him enthralled. His fascination may be mental. She may be the one who opens the occult world to him. The friendship can be a good one; luck prevails.

* * *

The following aspect starts April 11, 1975. It reaches a peak April 11, 1976 and leaves his chart April 11, 1977.

ASPECT: *MC progressed opposition Moon natal*

By progression, this is a highly discordant aspect. In his natal chart, there is a Trine aspect between the Moon and MC; therefore, this is a harmonious and discordant influence.

HOUSES INVOLVED: See page 113 for the Moon's influence. The natal MC is the 10th house cusp. The progressed MC is in the 11th house until February 26, 1976, at which time it will enter the 12th house.

Work

Travel and business can interfere with each other; also, with his family and friends. He will probably want to tend to them simultaneously, but can't. This conflict between these areas may disturb him. The constant see-saw continues bringing with it many separations, sacrifices and a choice to be made between two highly desirable areas. His final decision can prove lucky.

147

* * *

While on a trip, he is likely to take many papers which are necessary to study with him. Time is of the essence, and Nixon will possibly desire to work anywhere. Most of his labor is performed in his home or office, because of the quick conferences needed with people. This is why travel can be a nuisance to him during this time period.

* * *

The following applies if he's still President. A friend can offer him a highly desirable proposition. If Nixon accepts it, he may sacrifice his position and reputation. Bad publicity is likely to follow. The general populace and his aides will probably be against him.

NOTE: If he's not in public office, he may still attract the preceeding and the following events; replace the word "aide" for "help." On the other hand, Nixon may think that the deal with his buddy is tempting. It can possibly be financially rewarding. The more Nixon thinks about accepting or rejecting the project, the more confused he is likely to become.

As April 11, 1976 approaches, Nixon may have an emotional tug-of-war between his job and the friend's proposal. His health can be partly involved in his conflict. His final decision tends to prove fortunate.

* * *

Nixon may undergo some changes in business, travel or with his pals, family, employees and staff (if he's in power). Adverse talk and publicity may abound, if a buddy of Nixon's takes a trip with him or meets him along the way.

* * *

Flighty and impulsive behavior can cause Nixon difficulty now. If he makes too many quick changes, newspaper coverage might not be to his liking. Mixed public reactions may prevail.

* * *

While overseas, Nixon can be offered a fantastic business proposition. The person it comes from may be in a top and powerful position. The transaction proposed can involve an exchange. International trade may be part of the undertaking. This can be beneficial for everyone concerned, including Nixon's pals.

Time will probably lapse before Nixon makes a decision. All of the pros and cons will be weighed. Nixon's name, reputation and perhaps, his position may be necessary to take into account.

* * *

If he's still President, his staff and the public may not all agree to the facts as they are presented. If Nixon's out of office, repercussions with people may cause some difficulties in his final choice with this business proposal. However, luck is most likely to be in store for Nixon.

Court

A court case can be pending. A friend or staff member may be implicated. It's possible that Nixon is afraid the person will testify against him. At this time he may not know who to trust.

An ultimate break can occur with the individual. Changes may take place with the members of his staff. He could lose his job. However, there's possibly a last minute saving grace. Someone, including the general populace, may come to Nixon's aid. Perhaps, everyone's day will be filled with rumors and gossip.

NOTE: The first and second sentences in the preceding paragraph apply, if Nixon is still in public office.

* * *

The following aspect starts May 7, 1976. It reaches a peak June 7 and July 18, 1976. The aspect leaves his chart August 18, 1976.

ASPECT: *Moon progressed Semi-square Neptune (natal and progressed)*

By progression, this is a discordant aspect. In his natal chart, there is no aspect between these two planets; therefore, this is a discordant influence.

HOUSES INVOLVED: See page 113 for the Moon's influence. The natal Neptune is in the 11th house. The sign Pisces is on the 7th house cusp. (Neptune is one of the rulers of Pisces.)

Court

NOTE: The following may apply if a court case is pending.

Nixon will probably try to stall any legal proceedings. It's possible that he will attempt to escape from them with fibs, promises of favors to another, or bribery. However, at this time, there is no way out. He's likely to be led into a trap which his enemies arranged, or one which he weaved.

Lies, deceptions and trickery can hang in the courtroom air. Documents and records may have been falsified. Plots and schemes can be manufactured to disguise what has really transpired. Perhaps, everyone will deviate from the truth. People can be caught in the web of dishonesty which possibly prevails.

Nixon may talk in superlatives. He is liable to pretend that he knows nothing about the actual facts which are presented. His confusion may be so bad that he does not realize what he is saying. He may feel that he's in a fog because he doesn't know which way, or to whom, he can turn for him. Disappointments can reign. His hopes may be unrealized. A job or case may be lost. If so, he will most likely be in a daze. Nixon probably won't believe it's all happening to him.

The Public

Lies may be told. Promises made can be broken. Gossip will most likely be exaggerated. Whatever Nixon says, the public probably will not believe. His rating with them can be low. Perhaps, people are against him.

Business

An enormous undertaking can be his for the moment. However, the benefits promised may be made up or dramatized. He tends to be in a trusting mood. It's possible that he will be led astray. Changes may take place. All schemes can fizzle or fall short of what is promised. Nixon may be disappointed and annoyed with his friends, and the whole mess.

* * *

His pity and sympathy for a pal may lead him into some peculiar and bad ordeals. If the person smooth talks him into a partnership deal, it may not last. The individual can be insincere, or a hoax may be pulled. When the wrong doing is discovered, Nixon may be left holding the bag. If the buddy turns out to be an enemy, Richard will be shattered.

Foreign Relationships

If a huge project is started with those in other countries it will probably be unproductive. Any idealistic schemes of his will now possibly fall through. Frabrications may be bandied about by Nixon, his aides, partners or those in power overseas.

* * *

An individual who he has confided in and sworn by can now turn on him. Bribery, corruption and betrayal may be in the air. The sparks can fly. Changes may take place which might make Nixon peeved. The reason that the person may abandon him in a crisis is because of Nixon's broken promise, or an untruth. Richard can possibly be placed in a bad light now. The buck is likely to be passed back and forth. The public won't know who to believe.

* * *

If Nixon's still President, goods which are promised (like oil) may not be shipped. Others are liable to renege on their word. Importing and illegal items may be smuggled in. Contraband may be a problem. Nixon may be blamed for everything. The international drug traffic may possibly involve a friend, or acquaintance, of Nixon's.

Friends
Nixon may attract offers of overnight fortunes. Irritations can take place with the pals who have misrepresented business deals. Lies may be told to buddies, or they may fib to him. Disappointments can ensue. It's possible that a person he had once admired and respected has now fallen off of the pedestal. The awakening can be heartbreaking. Nixon probably won't feel like picking up the pieces, instead he may want to escape from the friendship.

Personal Concerns
It's possible that Nixon is going to tell his loved ones that he isn't going to work anymore. Perhaps, his mood is to retire and withdraw from the business world, and his cronies. To sit back, relax and daydream may be his longing. Possibly to travel around the world will be his utmost desire. However, any plans he makes at this time can be changed. If he does travel now, flying and sea voyages should be avoided.

* * *

Possibly any absentmindedness could be that Nixon's blocking unpleasant situations by living in a world which he has mentally created. However, if he is facing reality, he will probably be expecting the worst to happen.

* * *

Half-truths may, at the present time, be told to his wife. The fabrications will probably be in relationship to his business transactions here and abroad, court cases, and their friends.

* * *

His health can be a source of difficulty. Nixon is likely to be emotionally exhausted. Doctors may have trouble diagnosing any illness.

151

Food poisoning, pneumonia, germs, or bacteria substance can be attracted. Nixon may feel that he has sleeping sickness. It's possible that he's dizzy, in limbo, or a coma.

* * *

The following aspect starts July 21, 1976. It reaches a peak August 21, 1976 and leaves his chart September 21, 1976.

ASPECT: *Moon progressed Sextile Mercury progressed*
By progression, this is a harmonious aspect. In his natal chart, there is no aspect between these two planets: therefore, this is a harmonious influence.
HOUSES INVOLVED: See page 113 for the Moon's influence. The sign Virgo is on the 1st house cusp. (Mercury rules Virgo.) The natal Mercury is in the 4th house. The progressed Mercury is in the 7th house. The sign Gemini is on the 10th house cusp. (Mercury rules Gemini.)

Business

He can receive good service from employees, or his aides (if he's still in public office). They are likely to keep him up-to-date on the latest developments. There may be less errors made. Changes in personnel can take place which may benefit Nixon.

Favorable opportunities can now be attracted to sign papers, agreements, contracts and documents with foreign nations, or involving new laws, changes in procedure, or with real estate investments. The foregoing can apply regardless of whether he's the President or a businessman.

* * *

Nixon may feel that communication is vital. To talk and listen to others can possibly bring him favorable opportunities. His ideas are probably sound. Most likely his reasoning is good. Any logical deductions he makes may prove advantageous. Decisions can be easily made and well received.

* * *

His speech can be witty, intelligent and understandable. Press coverage couldn't be better, and interviews with reporters may be excellent. Nixon's beliefs and opinions will possibly go over now. The public will most likely accept what is said. Fans will probably be rooting for him.

152

* * *

This will be an auspicious time to discuss, or form, partnerships with friends. Real estate or foreign transactions are favored.

* * *

If Nixon is searching for a new home, or another piece of land, now is the time for him to act. Subconsciously, he may be thinking about making many good changes. Whether they are for the present, or future, his thoughts are now on the right track.

Foreign Relationships

Importing and exporting is favored. Ideas can be exchanged which will aid everyone concerned. The working class may approve of Nixon's deals.

* * *

Travel to far away places with his wife can be pleasant and interesting. Nixon's mind is likely to be open, receptive and active. As a result, many new avenues may be open to him. He should now seize them.

Court

If he had to appear before a judge or jury, an appeal to them through the spoken word will be in his favor.

* * *

The following aspect starts October 1, 1976. It reaches a peak November 1, 1976 and leaves his chart December 1, 1976.

ASPECT: *Moon progressed Inconjunct ASC progressed*

By progression, this is a neutral aspect. In his natal chart, it is also a neutral Inconjunct. With this type of an aspect neither harmony nor inharmony is felt. However, the influence can be harmonious or discordant dependent upon how Nixon utilizes it.

HOUSES INVOLVED: See page 113 for the Moon's influence. The natal ASC is the 1st house cusp. The progressed ASC is in the 3rd house.

Personal Concerns

Nothing much comes of the business offers attracted, unless he pushes them into action.

He tends to be in a blah mood. His personality doesn't come across too well at this time. People may not pay that much attention to him.

* * *

Nixon may meet with family and friends, others tend to bore him. He's rather restless. Any news that he receives will not likely be the cause of any upsets. He may want to discuss his personal affairs with someone, but may decide against it.

* * *

The following aspect starts December 15, 1976. It reaches a peak January 15, 1977 and leaves his chart February 15, 1977.

ASPECT: *Moon in a Conjunction to the MC*

By progression, this is a neutral aspect. In his natal chart, there is a Trine aspect between the Moon and the MC; therefore, this is a harmonious influence.

HOUSES INVOLVED: See page 113 for the Moon influence. The natal MC is the 10th house cusp. The progressed MC is in the 12th house.

NOTE: On January 15, 1977, Nixon's Moon will enter into his 10th house. This will bring about many changes in business for the following two years. Publicity and public opinion about him will continue to fluctuate. He will still, probably, be the center of the stage. Gossip can possibly flourish.

Nixon may receive auspicious publicity from December 15, 1976 to February 15, 1977. It's possible that people will hold him in high esteem. Press coverage can be excellent. This may be a lucky period for him. Offers in business can possibly come through friends, or those in powerful positions. Nixon may now announce his future plans. His reception is likely to be fantastic.